REFLECTING
GOD

Kay Smith

THE WORD
FOR TODAY

P.O. Box 8000, Costa Mesa, CA 92628 • Web Site: www.twft.com • E-mail: info@twft.com

Reflecting God
by Kay Smith
Edited by Shannon Woodward

Published by The Word For Today
P.O. Box 8000, Costa Mesa, CA 92628
Web site: http://www.twft.com
(800) 272-WORD (9673)

© 2009 The Word For Today

ISBN: 978-1-59751-090-5

Printed in the United States of America.

TABLE OF CONTENTS

INTRODUCTION

THE WORD "EXHORT" MEANS TO incite by argument or advice, and to give warnings or urgent appeals. I'm telling you this because I feel I should warn you right up front that I'm an exhortative teacher, and this is an exhortative book full of exhortative messages.

Now, my intention in writing this book is not to cause a riot. That's not the kind of inciting I'm after. "Incite" means to stir up and to spur to action. That's what I want.

My goal in writing this book is to spur you to become all that God desires and plans for you to be. Because as I look at Christian women today, I see that many of you know nothing at all about the abundant life you could be living. Many of you are oblivious of the life Jesus came to bring you. And because of this, the life you're living is less satisfying, less fulfilling, less joyful, and less God-honoring than it could be—than it *should* be.

Although the message of this book will stand alone, it could be considered a continuation of my first book, *Pleasing God*. Once you've settled in your mind that you want to please the Lord, then some things will naturally begin to take root in your life, and other things will begin to be uprooted because the Holy Spirit is at work. As you yield yourself to God and He starts dealing one by one with issues that are less than pleasing to Him, your life shines brighter and brighter. You begin to take on God's attributes, or characteristics. You begin to have the mind of Christ. As this starts to happen within you—outwardly, you become a reflection of God to a world that desperately needs Him.

When I first taught these lessons many years ago, the world seemed very dark and hopeless to me. All these years later, it has only become more so. These lessons are more timely today—but that doesn't mean they are any easier to hear. When I first announced that I would be teaching these lessons from the book of Titus, I heard some interesting comments from the young women who planned to attend the study. One came up to me with a strained, depressed expression and asked, "Kay, is your study just going to be about submitting to your husband?" Another young wife and mother wanted to know if I'd be teaching anything besides "staying home and taking care of the kids." You would have thought by their expressions that I had announced I would be serving them all a big plate of turnips.

Oh, how I hated turnips when I was a little girl. I couldn't help but gag when I saw those yucky things on my plate. And it wasn't just turnips—I hated most vegetables, and milk too. My poor mother! Can you imagine? She managed to get the milk in me by preparing custards and tapioca pudding, both of which I loved. But there's not much you can do to disguise a vegetable. Vegetables are going to taste like vegetables no matter what you do to them. So you know how my mother handled those? She put them on my plate and said, "Eat them. They're good for you." I needed them and she knew it, so that was that.

As you go through this book, you're going to find some things that you like and some things that you don't. You'll find some things you already agree with and other things you want to rebel against. If a little rebellion starts to show itself, that's all right—you just take it to Jesus. I have to do that myself now and again. Even as I studied this topic in preparation for my teaching, the Lord stepped on my toes a bit and said, "Now, Kay, shape up. This is the place where I want you to walk in a more circumspect way." My hope is that you'll experience that too. Think of those harder lessons as being your spiritual vegetables. They're good for you, and you need them, and that's that.

Throughout this study, we're going to look at a lot of Scripture. In particular, we're going to look closely at Paul's letter to Titus, in which he gave Titus clear direction about the things he was to do and to teach in his church. One of those instructions is specifically for you and me. The Holy Spirit inspired Paul to tell Titus of the importance of older women teaching or training the younger women (Titus 2:3-4).

At the point I find myself in life, I feel equipped to do that for you. Symbolically speaking, I've walked up ahead on the path. Have you ever been on a hike with someone, and one of your companions has walked on ahead? How comforting it is to hear a report back from one who has gone ahead. "Keep walking! It's not so bad up here ... in fact, it's beautiful! There's one pit in the road you'll want to watch out for, and there's a cactus up on the right, and some thorns there on the left, but once you see the view up here, you'll be glad you took every step!"

That's what this book is for. It's a guide to encourage you, to exhort you to walk in God's way—which is the very best way to walk—so you'll keep moving up the path. This path is the only one that offers joy, and the only path worth walking. The psalmist David said, "Show me Your ways, O LORD; teach me Your paths" (Psalm 25:4).

I want you to underline or highlight that verse and meditate on it as we go through these studies, because I do not want you to learn *my* ways—I want you to learn the *Lord's* ways. I do not want you to follow *my* paths—I want you to follow His paths. And I desire that for you because I want you to have the joyful, satisfying, abundant life God intends for you.

But too often, women settle for less. It's like one of my friends used to say: "You're spoiled to the world, but you haven't yet laid hold of the good things God has for you." That's a joyless place to be. If that's you today, I pray this book will stir you and spur you to grab hold of everything God has for you.

David understood the abundant life God wants to give us. He wrote, "At Your right hand are pleasures forevermore" (Psalm 16:11). When you've had a little taste of the pleasures of God, nothing this life offers can equal it. But those pleasures only come to those who walk in full commitment to Him. If you're walking with one foot in the world and one in the Lord, you're never going to know the deep fulfillment and joy God wants to give you.

As the time of Christ's return draws closer, we're going to see a much greater division between godly women and women of the world. Gray is rapidly disappearing and life is becoming starkly black and white—and all of us who call ourselves by His name must take a stand one way or the other. You're either a soldier of Christ or you're not. You're on the right path or you're on the wrong path. Now more than ever, it's vital that we commit ourselves to God and yield our lives to His Holy Spirit.

Ephesians 1:11-12 tells us,

> In Him also we have obtained an inheritance, being predestined according to the purpose of Him who works all things according to the counsel of His will, that we who first trusted in Christ should be to the praise of His glory.

God desires His children to proclaim and display His glory to a lost and dying world. That's what I want to do. I want people to look at my life and see a reflection of God's glory and splendor, His majesty and His might. I want them to look at my life and catch a glimpse of hope.

And I want them to see it in your life too.

As for me,
I will see Your face in righteousness;
I shall be satisfied when I awake
in Your likeness.

PSALM 17:15

Isn't that just the way life is? When we separate ourselves from the world and see life with God's divine perspective, we don't want any part of the sin that permeates the world. But when we lose that perspective and begin to walk amidst the world's pollution, we forget how poisonous and awful it is. We think wrongly, *Oh, it's not so bad.*

My heart's desire for you—and certainly God's desire for you—is that you'll be able to see yourself from His high perspective. You'll see the purity He wants you to have in your life and it will make you hate the poison and filth of the world.

Do you ever stop to consider what your position is as a redeemed child of God? The Word tells us that Jesus is the King of kings. He's the most high King—no one is greater. So if He is the King, and you've been adopted as His child, what does that make you? It makes you the King's daughter.

Psalm 45:13 tells us, "The king's daughter is all glorious within: her clothing is of wrought gold" (*KJV*). This is a description of you, if you belong to Jesus. You're the daughter of the King, and He has made you all glorious. He has clothed you with garments of righteousness.

Colossians 3 talks about the new garments we've been given through Christ.

> But now you yourselves are to put off all these: anger, wrath, malice, blasphemy, filthy language out of your mouth. Do not lie to one another, since you have put off the old man with his deeds, and have put on the new man who is renewed in knowledge according to the image of Him who created him (Colossians 3:8-10).

When we came to Jesus Christ, He came to dwell within us by His Holy Spirit. He did away with the old nature and gave us a new nature—He gave us His own.

MY FAIR LADY

I have always loved the musical *My Fair Lady*. [1] I think what is so captivating about it is that most of us, at one time or another, have wanted to be something other than what we are. I used to think, *Wouldn't it be wonderful to wake up beautiful and have my closet filled with all the right clothes? My annunciation and my diction would be perfect, and I'd be comfortable at any time in any situation, knowing I had it all together.* We never seem to be satisfied.

The musical is centered on the life of Eliza Doolittle, a flower girl down in the slums of London. She has this thick cockney accent and she's coarse and unrefined and all shabby-looking and tattered around the edges. Along comes Professor Henry Higgins and he makes a bet with his friend that he can spiff up Eliza so that he can take her any place in high society and they wouldn't recognize her background. Eliza agrees to the experiment and moves into Professor Higgins' house.

Now, the very first event in Eliza's transformation is a bath—which she needs badly. Professor Higgins turns her over to the housekeeper and she gets bathed from head to toe. Once she's clean, she's dressed in brand new clothing. After she sees herself in her beautiful new clothes, she holds up her old street clothes and asks, "What shall I do with these?" But there's nothing to do except burn them.

There's such a clear parallel between this story and our lives in Christ. When we've been cleansed by the blood of the Lamb and clothed in His robe of righteousness, there's nothing left to do with the old nature but to discard it completely.

As the story of *My Fair Lady* progresses, Eliza works harder and harder to learn how to be a lady. The professor demands a great deal from her and pushes her firmly. And even though she feels like giving up, eventually something happens—she changes. Not only that, she begins to fall in love with Professor Higgins. When that happens, the work she does is not to gain his respect or approval, nor is it done to earn the admiration of society. She does it out of her pure love for him.

Now, Henry Higgins is not the Lord Jesus Christ. For one thing, he was a real taskmaster, and for another, he didn't have eyes to see when Eliza began to love him. Every analogy breaks down someplace, and this one certainly breaks down on this point. Still, there's a beautiful parallel to our life in Christ. I want to be His fair lady—lovely within and without. I know you do too. And these verses will help spiff us up to be what we ought to be, to have that Christlike character that so pleases His heart and reflects Him to the world.

SPIRITUAL RENEWAL

Ephesians 4:17-19 gives us a good picture of the way we should not be walking as cleansed, newly robed brides of Christ:

> You should no longer walk as the rest of the Gentiles walk, in the futility of their mind, having their understanding darkened, being alienated from the life of God, because of the ignorance that is in them, because of the blindness of their heart; who, being past feeling, have given themselves over to lewdness, to work all uncleanness with greediness.

That's what we're to avoid. We're to stop walking as the heathens do and start walking as beautiful, cleansed, and renewed brides. We've been cleansed to walk with and for the Lord.

Paul goes on to say,

> But you have not so learned Christ, if indeed you have heard Him and have been taught by Him, as the truth is in Jesus: that you put off, concerning your former conduct, the old man which grows corrupt according to the deceitful lusts, and be renewed in the spirit of your mind, and that you put on the new man which was created according to God, in true righteousness and holiness (Ephesians 4:20-24).

"Be renewed in the spirit of your mind." I pray that those words are emblazoned on your heart. Being renewed is a continual action. It's not a once-and-for-all thing—it's moment by moment. In this smoggy world in which we're living, we need our minds renewed every day.

In the very first verse of Ephesians chapter 4, Paul exhorts us to "walk worthy of the calling with which you were called." To walk worthy of the calling we've been given means that we no longer copy the behavior of the world, which proves what Paul called the "futility of their mind" in verse 17. In the Greek it is translated as "the mind which fails to produce the desired result." Their purposeless lives are wasted on absolute nothingness.

Paul goes on to describe the downward spiral of the hardened heart. Now, you may have looked at that description and thought, *Oh, boy, I was just like that.* Or you may have looked at that description and thought, *I was never like that. I wasn't lascivious, I wasn't wicked, and I didn't have a hard heart.* Only you and the Lord know what your condition was before you came to Him. Hardness of heart comes through indulgence in sins that sears a conscience to the truth that is in Jesus Christ. Through continuous rejection of Jesus Christ and indulgence in sin, the heart of the unconverted person becomes harder and harder.

WHERE DOES SIN START?

Romans 1:18-32 is the perfect parallel to this passage in Ephesians, and actually describes that downward spiral in greater detail. I think every Christian should read Romans 1 over and over and over. We learn in Romans 1 that all of us are without excuse because nature reveals God. But because people do not honor God in their heart or glorify Him, and because they do not accept Him but instead continue in rejection and in sin, their foolish hearts are darkened.

We read that,

> And even as they did not like to retain God in their knowledge, God gave them over to a debased mind, to do those things which are not fitting (Romans 1:28).

At the very beginning, when all this trouble with sin began, where did it start for Eve? It started in her mind. Satan worked on her mind. He lied to her about God and planted doubts about Him in her thoughts. In the end, she listened to those lies and chose to indulge in pleasure rather than obey God.

That's still Satan's playground today. Sin always starts in the mind. It's possible that you're struggling right now against the subtle (or not so subtle) lies of the enemy. I pray this is not so. But if that is the case, you need to know you're in a precarious position. You must stand firm on what you know to be true and fight with all that is in you against the lies of the enemy.

When we talk about addictions, many people distance themselves from the conversation because they don't feel it applies to them. You can talk to someone about how easy it is to become enslaved to alcohol, cocaine or prescription drugs, and they'll nod and agree with you. You can tell they see themselves as being "above" that temptation.

But did you know the same rush, the same excitement, the same satisfaction that some people get from drugs or alcohol is what draws women into promiscuity or adulterous affairs? Women who would never touch drugs or take any other kind of mind-altering substance can be enslaved by the passions of the mind and heart.

Just like the one who becomes trapped by a substance, the woman caught in sexual sin is on the same downward spiral. Her addiction hardens her heart and causes her to deny the life of God within her. Unless something drastic happens to cause such a one to denounce her sin and turn back to God, her ending will be tragic.

Isaiah 44:20 says,

> He feeds on ashes; a deceived heart has turned him aside; and he cannot deliver his soul, nor say, "Is there not a lie in my right hand?"

Dear sister, you must be ever alert to the tactics of the enemy. Don't get caught up in his lies. Look around at how pervasive evil is in our world and be that much more vigilant to keep yourself pure. In case you haven't noticed, our world has gone completely crazy.

FILTHY MCNASTY

Years ago, Chuck and I were in Hawaii and he was reading the newspaper one morning. After a bit, I saw him put the paper down and shake his head. He had that look on his face, the one that said he'd just read something disgusting or disturbing.

I said, "Honey, what?"

He began to tell me about the article he'd just read. It seemed a woman had sued the Salvation Army because they fired her. And why did they fire her? Because she had been caught copying Wiccan material on their copiers. She was a witch, and she was using the Salvation Army's equipment to copy her pagan material. Of course, they didn't know she was a witch when they hired her.

Unbelievably, the courts had found in favor of the witch! The Salvation Army was forced to pay her a large sum of money to compensate for firing her. Chuck and I were both so saddened by that.

It was just more proof that the world we live in is governed by the prince of the power of the air. Later that day, we were walking along the street

watch these movies. Now, some of you are forced to watch these movies with your husbands. I understand that, and I'm very empathetic and sympathetic to you. But my heart grieves over any woman who would voluntarily watch ungodly and immoral movies in a theater today. I'm not going to stand outside any theater and judge you. If I see you walking in, don't say, "Oh, no, Kay saw me." That doesn't matter. It's not important that I see you. It's important that the Lord Jesus Christ sees you.

If you're living your life to please God, you must hold every activity out with an open hand and be willing for Him to take it if that thing needs to go. And if we desire to live a life that reflects Jesus to others, we need to ask if the activity we're about to do is in keeping with His character. Would Jesus go to see and be entertained by the filth in the theaters? You know the answer to that.

When we who have God's Spirit living within us finally see what the world is really like, when our eyes are wide open to the source behind the world's entertainment, its customs, its fashions, its laws, its relationships and its lifestyles—there should be such an attitude of repulsion in our hearts that we absolutely have no desire to walk in it, to be entertained by it, or to adapt any part of it.

GOD'S PERSPECTIVE

We need to read Ephesians 4:17-19 over and over, and we need to read Romans 1:18-32 until it finally sinks in.

> For this reason God gave them up to vile passions. For even their women exchanged the natural use for what is against nature. Likewise also the men, leaving the natural use of the woman, burned in their lust for one another, men with men committing what is shameful ... God gave them over to a debased mind, to do those things which are not fitting; being filled with all unrighteousness, sexual immorality, wickedness, covetousness, maliciousness; full of envy, murder, strife, deceit, evil-mindedness;

they are whisperers, backbiters, haters of God, violent, proud, boasters, inventors of evil things, disobedient to parents, undiscerning, untrustworthy, unloving, unforgiving, unmerciful … (Romans 1:26-31).

Is that not a horrid list? Even though you're likely not doing all those vile things, the fact is, you're living in a world that is filled with them. Each one is a potential trap. As daughters of the King and as the bride of Christ, we must keep ourselves from the world's filth. We must discover and embrace God's perspective through a diligent study of His Word. Then the world and all its charm will lose its grip on us.

I'll tell you, if you were a pastor's wife, it wouldn't take very long before you would hate this world system as I do. We see wrecked lives week after week after week. When Christians adopt the world's behavior, they suffer the world's devastation.

Not long ago I saw two men who used to walk with Jesus but now have abandoned Him for this world. One is addicted to cocaine and the other is enslaved by something else equally horrible. They come around once in a while and it's plain to see they want to get free. They really do. So we will gather some intercessors to pray for them, and for a little while they will walk in that freedom and experience the joy of fellowship with Jesus. But then it isn't long before they begin entertaining a little bit of the world here, a little bit there. Before you know it, they're enslaved all over again.

I see that same story over and over. I can't tell you the countless number of marriages that have been destroyed by drugs and alcohol and by illicit affairs, or the number of times I've watched mothers leave their children and run to the world. It's absolutely heartbreaking. And it's terrifying because what we see at the end of Ephesians 4:19 is sin's final effect—to anesthetize the conscience, to take it to a point where the person no longer has any feeling about sin.

I don't like reading these dark sections of Scripture any more than you do. I'm a devotional reader. I just want to read things that will help me to develop my friendship with Jesus Christ. I want to worship Him and wait for Him to speak to me and say, "This is the path you're to walk on today." I want to be like a watered garden full of fragrance, and I don't want the stench of the old life around me at all. But God has said, "Kay, you've got to know My viewpoint and My perspective of this world—friendship with it is hostility toward Me."

THE BATTLE FOR YOUR MIND

A choice stands before each one of us. We make a one-time decision to reject the world and choose Jesus when we bow before Him and ask forgiveness for our sins. But that decision must be renewed daily. He made you a new creature—what will you do with this new day? Do you want friendship with God today or friendship with the world? Which is more important to you? If fellowship with God is more important, then obedience is the price—obedience to God's Word and obedience in letting go of all that is contrary to His character.

I think sometimes Christians forget they've been born again and that they're brand-new creatures. Instead of walking in the Spirit, they walk in the flesh, and they let all the old trash from their past life control what they do today. That's what happens when you walk in the flesh. Traumas from long ago rise up and try to control you all over again. I hardly know a person who wasn't traumatized by something they could blame all their mistakes on. No one escapes this life without some of those things. But you don't have to let them control you. You can walk in the freedom you have as a new creature in Christ.

I want you to really absorb this truth: You have been created in the likeness of God—in the likeness of God Himself. Not only that, but 2 Peter 1:4 tells us—and this makes me breathless—that we are "partakers of His divine nature." There's no nature anywhere that you could admire more than His. Jesus is gentle, loving, compassionate, merciful, kind, long-suffering, and just. We are partakers of that divine nature. He is the truth! And when we embrace and accept that truth, then the fullness of truth comes into our lives. How precious that promise is—how wonderful!

The Word teaches us that because we belong to Christ, we have the mind of Christ (1 Corinthians 2:16). That means the work of His Holy Spirit within us transforms our thinking and our reasoning. Our will conforms to His. Our desires line up with His desires. No longer are we trapped in the darkness of our own ignorance and faulty reasoning. What was obscured becomes clear.

But—and this is where you must really sit up and listen—the battle for your mind is not over. It's as intense as ever. Satan is constantly studying you and looking for sneaky ways he can infiltrate your mind. That's why Ephesians 4:23 is written in the active tense: "Be renewed in the spirit of your mind." We must actively offer ourselves to the Holy Spirit to be renewed and directed by Him. The alternative is to let the world sway us. If you don't offer yourself to the Holy Spirit's influence and control, you can be sure that TV, worldly magazines and all the rest will be only too happy to fill your mind with its filth.

RENEW YOUR MIND

Fight it, dear one. I'm fighting right along with you. My friend, Carolyn Lamb, used to say, "I work to stay pure." That's such a wise statement. Are you working to stay pure? Are you diligent to keep yourself untarnished by the world? It isn't easy—not for any of us. All of us are susceptible to temptation, and the world is full of things that will attract you and me—little shiny mirrors that try to draw us away. Usually they're not big things, because Satan is smart enough to disguise small sins so we're unguarded. As Satan tempted Eve, "It's nothing important … just a little fruit, that's all. What difference will one little bite, one little indulgence make?" Satan is willing to start small because he knows a tiny foothold today will lead to a big sin down the road. But we don't have to lose that battle. James 4:7 says, "Resist the devil and he will flee from you."

So how is your mind continually renewed? It happens through prayer and through the reading of God's Word. That's how you daily gain the mind of Christ. Colossians 3:16 tells us, "Let the word of Christ dwell in you richly." Oh, the Word of God renews my mind. When I'm really upset about something, I go to the Word. "Oh God, give me a Scripture." I say, "Quicken a Scripture to my heart that will solve this, that I might be obedient to You so I will not walk in the flesh and do something that would disappoint You or grieve Your Holy Spirit." And God is always so faithful to do just that. But it takes great determination, diligence, and watchfulness to keep your mind renewed. You have to be willing to be a gatekeeper, watching closely to see what you're allowing in.

I remember years ago when Janette, my oldest daughter, went through a battle with her girls over a television series based on the story of *Beauty and the Beast*. They were showing it at eight o'clock one night and she let them watch the first episode. In fact, she watched it with them. She said it was very sweet and harmless. But then the next week, she happened to catch a preview of that week's episode. In the original cartoon version, there was no sexual entanglement or anything inappropriate.

But in this television version, the preview showed a new man coming into Beauty's life—and lo and behold, they had a bedroom scene together. Now, this was being shown at eight o'clock in the evening, when little children would be watching. Do you see how the world is trying to shape their value system and fill them with curiosity? When I was younger, I never saw anything overtly stimulating like what they show regularly on TV now.

My mother had some books that she wouldn't let me near, but they weren't bad. I know because I found a way to look at them, curious little brat that I was. They were nursing books that showed the proper way to bandage a wound, and then a few other things I probably shouldn't have seen. They were so clinically-oriented, they wouldn't stimulate anybody. But nevertheless, I was curious. And look what children are being stimulated by now. Oh, the commercials on TV are so wicked, I can hardly bear them.

FIGHT EVIL AND STAY STRONG

So back to Janette. She told me when she saw what the upcoming episode would include, she told the girls, "No *Beauty and the Beast* this week. In fact, no more *Beauty and the Beast* at all."

The kids didn't like it. "Why not? I like that show!" Your kids will do the same. But you're not there to be popular with your children, right? You're there to hear from God and hold them to the line.

Janette brought out a video about the life of Jesus they could watch instead. Her daughter, Brittany, was five at the time, and after Brittany had been watching it for a bit, she came down to the kitchen where Janette was and she said, "Mom, I'm sadder than I've ever been in my whole life."

Janette said, "Honey, what in the world is the matter?"

Brittany cried, "They killed Jesus. They killed Jesus."

Something about seeing that video had broken through to Brittany. When Janette told me about her comment, I asked, "Has Brittany received Jesus into her heart?"

Janette told me that she had done it when she was three, but then she added, "Mom, the Lord's done a deeper work." So we decided it might be time to pray again. So Janette and Brittany had a talk about what happened on the cross, and about how Jesus paid for all her sins with His death. They prayed together, and my little granddaughter asked Jesus into her heart again—this time, with a greater understanding. And all because her mom was strong enough to say no to *Beauty and the Beast*.

Now, I'm not telling you that you must limit yourself to watching videos about Jesus. That's not what I'm saying. I'm not trying to paralyze you with legalism to the point where you feel like you can't move or breathe. I feel so free in Jesus Christ! I can do anything I want to do. I've heard it said, "Love Christ and do what you will." When you really love Jesus, you don't want to sin at all. But I am saying that you must be selective about what you allow to enter your mind, and the minds of your little ones.

Oh, beloved, is it worth it? Yes, yes, yes. Be alert and on guard. Be the new creation you are in Christ, created in righteousness and holiness. Remember who you are: His beautiful bride. "The king's daughter is all glorious within. Her garments are of woven gold." You've been cleansed from head to foot and robed in pure garments. Your old rags have been burned. Leave them in the burn pile. Don't go poking around in there. And don't look back—not for a second. Instead, live a lifestyle that corresponds to your new nature and your position—as God's fair lady.

Father, our heart's desire is to be like Jesus. May we take hold of the truth of Your Word, and may we become living examples of Your nature. Give us Your divine perspective, Lord, that we would clearly see the traps the enemy tries to lay at our feet. Keep us pure. Keep us set apart for You.

In the precious name of Jesus we ask. Amen.

2

SHE IS CLOTHED IN BEAUTY

IN OUR LAST CHAPTER we talked about the fact that when we came to Jesus, He cleansed us, dressed us in His royal garments, and burned our old, filthy rags. I want to look at that more closely, because in our quest to portray God to the world around us, what we choose to wear is vital.

Clothing is a funny thing. It's just fabric and thread, you know, but it can really affect our mood. If we're wearing something that's comfortable and becoming, we feel good. Other times we quickly grab something out of the closet, throw it on, and run out the door. Later we look down and think, *Why on earth did I wear this? I've never liked it. I've never felt good in it. Why didn't I get rid of this a long time ago?* Or we leave the house feeling pretty good until we catch sight of ourselves in a mirror or a store window and we think, *Oh, my word. I look awful.*

I remember way back when those droopy, frumpy dresses were very popular. Fortunately, that style didn't remain popular for long. But I went out and bought one of those dresses without even trying it on. Everybody gasped when they saw it on me. It wasn't a winner. I couldn't do a thing to improve it. No scarf or necklace hid the fact that it was truly an awful dress.

We can usually pick up clues to a person's personality and attitude about life by the way they dress. Some women dress outrageously or provocatively to attract attention. Other styles of dress are designed to make a statement. The hippies definitely did that. Long hair doesn't mean the same thing today, but back then if you saw a boy with long hair, you knew he was making a statement against society. Some people became really incensed over that.

We used to have a friend who never tied his shoestrings and almost never wore socks. He always looked like he had just grabbed any old thing out of his closet without paying too much attention to what it was. He was a brilliant thinker and his head was always in the clouds. I guess when you're busy thinking great thoughts, you don't have time to tie your shoestrings, do you?

BIBLICAL CHARACTER DRESSING

You might be surprised at how often the Bible talks about clothing. Passage after passage deals with this subject. In Genesis, Adam and Eve tried to clothe themselves after they disobeyed God and became aware of their nakedness. Before they partook of the tree of the knowledge of good and evil, they didn't have a shameful opinion of their nakedness. It wasn't sinful to them. But once they bit into that fruit, they saw themselves in a whole different light, and they tried to sew aprons made of fig leaves. But God had to step in and make clothing for them. It required the first blood sacrifice. In order to cover their nakedness—their shame—an animal had to die which was, of course, symbolic of the sacrifice Jesus would make when He came to earth.

Later in Genesis, Jacob wore sackcloth as a sign of mourning when he thought Joseph had been killed by wild beasts. Sackcloth was a coarse, uncomfortable type of fabric people wore to show their grief or repentance.

I remember once when Chuck and I were invited to a wild church where the minister had announced beforehand he would be wearing sackcloth. Sure enough, when we showed up and took a seat, there he was on the stage—clothed in that scratchy burlap. We thought, *This should be interesting.* But then at one point he raised his hands to praise the Lord and we could clearly see the silk lining under the burlap. Cheater!

There's also an account in 2 Kings 6:30 about one of Israel's kings who, in response to the horrible effects of a famine, walked along the city walls wearing his robe. But in his grief he had torn his clothing, and as he passed by, the people could see a glimpse of the sackcloth he wore underneath.

Have you ever done that? Have you ever gone out among people and on the outside everything seems fine, but emotionally underneath it all you were wearing sackcloth because you were hurting or mourning over something?

I could go on for a long time pointing out verses which talk about clothing. But I'd like to focus on three passages that are of great importance to those who are walking with Jesus. These passages are in Colossians, 1 Peter, and Isaiah.

As we go through the Scriptures, I want you to visualize yourself being clothed with the things that are desirable and discarding the things that are not. We're going to clean out our spiritual closet, so to speak. We don't want even one garment remaining that will cause confusion in the eyes of those who are watching us. We want all who come into contact with us to know clearly who we belong to, and what we stand for.

This idea of casting off undesirable clothing comes straight from Colossians 3:8. As stated in *The Living Bible*, it says,

> Cast off and throw away all these rotten garments of anger, hatred, cursing, and dirty language.

Those are definitely garments you want to get rid of. Who would want to go out into the world wearing anger or hatred? Jude 23 adds a descriptive thought about such garments. It says, "… hating even the garment defiled by the flesh." Any garment that is in any way spotted by the flesh needs to go. We need to loathe such a garment. Out of curiosity, I studied this verse to see exactly what it meant. It's referring to a passage in the Old Testament about the leper. Once the leper was cleansed and healed, all the clothes he had ever worn were to be burned. This was done to get rid of the disease.

Now, we know leprosy in the Bible is a symbol of sin. God was telling them to hate the clothes that were contaminated by this disease. As Christians, we should have a perfect hatred for these attitudes of the flesh that stain our garments as daughters of the King, keeping us from being the representatives and the reflection of our Father that we ought to be.

SPIRITUAL GARMENTS

Colossians 3:12, 14 in the *New International Version* says,

> Therefore, as God's chosen people, holy and dearly loved, clothe yourselves with compassion, kindness, humility, gentleness and patience …

And over all these virtues put on love, which binds them all together in perfect unity.

That's the kind of layered look you want with love coordinating it all.

Take a moment to check that list: compassion, kindness, humility, gentleness and patience. Is this how you dressed today? Were you more interested in these spiritual garments or your material clothing? As the King's daughter, did you take time to adorn yourself with things that last eternally? You should probably post a little sign on the bathroom mirror that says, "Today I will adorn myself for the Lord."

These verses clearly tell you that some of this is your responsibility. You have a choice about how you adorn yourself. But the foundational part of this is God's responsibility. Before you can make those choices for yourself, you must first have a right relationship with Jesus.

If you do not know Jesus—if He is not your Savior—you could try to put these things on, but it wouldn't ring true. True compassion, true kindness, humility, gentleness and patience can come only from Him. Jesus gives you the ability to choose those garments but you still have to make the choice. You can choose to dress yourself in anger, bitterness, resentment or fear. But if you want to make a choice that reflects God, you will discard those things and instead clothe yourself with the beautiful garments He makes available to you.

THE BEAUTY OF HUMILITY

The second passage comes from 1 Peter 5:5 which tells us to:

Be clothed with humility, for God resists the proud, but gives grace to the humble.

There's a big difference between genuine humility and false humility. Those who are truly humble are actually unconscious of it. Sometimes people will try to act humble by pretending they're not good at things they really are good at, but that's not humility. Humility is not an inferiority complex and it's not low self-esteem, nor is it the pretense of those things. True humility esteems others as being worthwhile, regardless of their station in life. It's a reflection of the humility Jesus had.

Philippians 2:5-8 says,

> Let this mind be in you which was also in Christ Jesus, who, being in the form of God, did not consider it robbery to be equal with God, but made Himself of no reputation, taking the form of a bondservant, and coming in the likeness of men. And being found in appearance as a man, He humbled Himself and became obedient to the point of death, even the death of the cross.

Jesus was willing to leave the beauty of heaven and come down to earth to die a painful death—all because He valued each and every life trapped in sin.

I remember Chuck's mom telling me once, "Kay, everyone you meet has something to teach you that you need to know." Isn't that good advice? I've found her words to be true. You can learn something from every person you meet. Unless you esteem each person as having value, though, you'll miss that lesson.

But even more than just esteeming others as having value, the Word tells us that we're to go a step further.

> Do nothing out of selfish ambition or vain conceit, but in humility consider others better than yourselves (Philippians 2:3 NIV).

It's not enough to say that other people have value. We have to get to the place where we consider others to have more value than we do. That can be difficult. Certainly, our society doesn't teach that at all. We're taught to size one another up and look for all the places where you're better than the other person. The truth is, there's only one whom we're to compare ourselves to, and that is Jesus. When we do that, like Isaiah, we will be compelled to utter, "Oh, I am unclean!" (Isaiah 6:5).

It's only when we compare ourselves with Jesus that we see our true condition. And that's the heart of humility. That is what allows you to esteem everyone else as being better than yourself.

Theologian Jonathan Edwards once preached a sermon entitled, "Sinners in the Hands of an Angry God." [2] It was so powerful, so convicting, that people crawled towards the altar to accept Christ. Edwards said, "Nothing sets a person so much out of the devil's reach as humility." If there isn't any pride in you to draw from, Satan has an awfully hard time tempting you, doesn't he? The proud person never sees his own sins, but God resists the proud and gives grace to the humble. Have you met people like that—people who feel they are spotless? Those people can't see their own sins, but they have an easy time pointing out the sins of others.

Where does humility come from? Noted Christian author, Andrew Murray said, "This humility is not a thing that will come of itself … it must be made the object of special desire and prayer and faith and practice." [3] Isn't that beautiful? If you make humility an object of desire, faith and prayer, and you consciously practice it in your life, it will become an unconscious beauty in your life.

Malcolm Muggeridge was once a guest on a TV program along with another man. Malcolm Muggeridge was a brilliant man and a terrific speaker, who could explain a concept so clearly that you could actually see it in your mind. But this other guest was not quite so gifted, although he didn't seem to know it himself. The way he spoke and handled himself made him seem like a bit of a know-it-all, although he wasn't nearly as educated or well-spoken as Malcolm Muggeridge. As I watched the conversation going back and forth, Malcolm began to say some really beautiful things—things that made me want to hear more. But the other man kept interrupting him and saying things that were not beautiful or edifying. It was frustrating to watch.

But then Malcolm turned to the man, looked at him with deep interest, and began to draw him out. What I saw in that was an example of true humility. I have no doubt that whatever Malcolm would have said would have been much more profound and more edifying, but he had the humility to step back and take second place. It was beautiful to watch, and something I'll never forget. It helps me to remember that every person we meet has eternal worth.

A CLOTHING ASSISTANT

The third passage I want to look at is in Isaiah 61:10, which says,

> I will greatly rejoice in the LORD, my soul shall be joyful in my God; for He has clothed me with the garments of salvation, He has covered me with the robe of righteousness, as a bridegroom decks himself with ornaments, and as a bride adorns herself with her jewels.

What I love about this verse is that it tells us our spiritual clothing isn't left up to us.

Haven't you ever wished for a personal clothing assistant—someone to come in and pick out all the clothes you would need for a season? You'd open your closet and there it would be—everything you need. I'd like that. I'd even like to have someone come into my house every morning and say, "This is what you will wear today." When I was a little girl I used to be fascinated by those movies where a maid would come in and lay out all the clothing on the bed. I'd think, *Oh, I'd love for someone to get all my clothes ready like that.*

The good news is that spiritually God has done just that for us. Read that verse again: "He has clothed me with the garments of salvation, He has covered me with the robe of righteousness." How do you like the clothing the Lord has laid out for you today? Do you feel like a bride with her jewels? You should, because your heavenly Father has clothed you with salvation and righteousness. That's what makes it possible for you to clothe yourself with humility, compassion and kindness.

The Living Bible puts Isaiah 61:10 this way,

> Let me tell you how happy God has made me. For He has clothed me with garments of salvation, and draped about me the robe of righteousness. I am like a bridegroom in his wedding suit, or a bride with her jewels.

A GARMENT OF PRAISE

Salvation and righteousness would be enough, but God has also clothed us with a "garment of praise for the spirit of heaviness" (Isaiah 61:3). Isn't that precious? The *NIV* says, "a garment of praise instead of a spirit of despair." Have you been wearing a spirit of despair? Did you get up this morning thinking, *Oh, I just can't make it through this day?* Well, did you know that you have been given all you need to get through this day? It's true.

Psalm 18:32-33 tells us,

> It is God who arms me with strength, and makes my way perfect. He makes my feet like the feet of deer, and sets me on my high places.

God has promised to give you hinds' feet on high places. And you need to realize there's not a craggy hill that you have to climb that He hasn't already prepared for you. Jesus has given you the sure-footedness of a mountain goat. You can get to the top of the mountain and scale the craggy peak today.

But even more than being able to do it—to go forth with the garment of praise instead of the spirit of heaviness—we should want to do it because it is not God's intention that we constantly walk about with a spirit of heaviness and despair. Do you know why He puts a garment of praise on you?

Isaiah 61:3 says,

> That they may be called trees of righteousness, the planting of the LORD, that He may be glorified.

We are the planting of the Lord. We are the trees of righteousness God has planted. What do people think when they see a tree that is all droopy and withered? Does that tree look cared for? Does it bring glory to the person who planted it? No. It looks like it's got a pretty bad gardener, doesn't it? Is that the testimony we want to shine forth to the world? Of course it isn't. But when we take the garment of praise God has given us, we look like beautiful, healthy, well-tended trees. We bring glory to His name.

We want everything we do to bring credit to our King. That's what it means to reflect Him to the world. When the world looks at us, they should see how cared for and loved we are. Our attitude should convey that to all who are watching.

As a little girl, my very favorite fairytale was *Cinderella*. I liked everything about it, even the wicked stepmother and the bad sisters. I could just see poor Cinderella down by the fireplace stoking the ashes and hearing, "Cinderella! Mop the floor!" But then along comes this fairy godmother who cleans up Cinderella and clothes her in a beautiful gown. Cinderella, of course, meets and marries the prince and they head off at the end of the story to live happily ever after. But what if Cinderella, after being rescued from her drudgery and clothed in beauty, had become a snobbish, imperious, haughty, proud woman? The story would be ruined, wouldn't it? We wouldn't like Cinderella and we wouldn't like that fairytale.

Well, that really is just a fairytale. But our life in Christ is reality. We *are* born again. We *are* daughters of a King. When we forget that—when we go about clothed in the garments of righteousness, salvation and praise that He's given us, but we also carry about anger, bitterness and despair—the world fails to see the beauty of Christ in us.

CLOTHE YOUR ATTITUDE

Take a moment to consider all that Jesus has done for you. Doesn't that make you want to clothe yourself in qualities of compassion, kindness, gentleness and humility? Those things are all attitudes. You can choose to esteem others as greater than yourself. You can choose to treat people kindly, gently, and with compassion.

It comes back again to guarding your mind. When those wrong, ugly attitudes begin to creep in, you must bring them to the Lord and ask Him to handle them for you.

Second Corinthians 10:5 reads, we must "bring every thought into captivity to the obedience of Christ." If you feel angry, tell the Lord that. If you feel bitter, tell the Lord. But then ask Him to take those stained, ragged, unbecoming garments from you.

Tell the Lord how much it matters to you to be a true representative for Him, a true reflection of His beauty to the world. He'll do it for you. You'll be able to tell by your reaction the next time you run into that person you were angry with or bitter toward. God will give you the ability to treat that person with love, but you have to choose in that moment which garment you will wear.

Will you choose the beautiful things He has provided for you, or will you choose garments that rightfully should be taken out, destroyed and burned?

Father, we deeply long to be a true reflection of You in this world. Help us to clean out our spiritual closets today. Take every ugly, stained, unbecoming attitude and remove it far from us. And remind us daily, Lord, of the beauty You have given us through the precious blood of Your Son. Conform us to Your image.

We ask all this in Your precious name. Amen.

CHAPTER

3

SHE IS HOLY

[Teach] the aged women likewise, that they be in behavior as becometh holiness, not false accusers, not given to much wine, teachers of good things; that they may teach the young women to be sober, to love their husbands, to love their children, to be discreet, chaste, keepers at home, good, obedient to their own husbands, that the word of God be not blasphemed (Titus 2:3-5 *KJV*).

IF YOU'RE A YOUNG WOMAN, it's easy to read that verse and assume it doesn't apply to you. But it does. Because unless the Lord comes back soon or He takes you home in death, you're going to become an older woman one of these days. When I was a young woman in my early twenties, I didn't think I would ever become that "older woman." But the years have gone by pretty fast, and before I knew it, I was a grandma—and then a great-grandma!

Back in my younger days, I had some pretty specific ideas about holiness and the kind of women who were "holy." If you had asked me back then, I could have rattled off a list of adjectives with no trouble whatsoever. In my mind, a holy woman was drab and dull. She never wore any makeup or attractive clothes. She was sour and cross-looking and didn't have a sense of humor. She was boringly pious and always disapproving—always wrathful, prudish, and completely undesirable. In other words, she was everything you wouldn't want to be.

Remember those old western shows on TV? If you recall, they always had one girl who lived in the saloon. She was "that kind of gal," but she was gorgeous, compassionate, tolerant, and desirable. She had a heart of gold and everyone loved her. But then there was this other woman—the one who wore a buttoned-up, high-collared dress and a hat. She had tight lips and no makeup, and carried an umbrella in her hand, ready to strike anybody who got too near. This was supposed to be the holy woman—the Christian.

Hollywood sent a subtle message to women: The harlot is much more attractive than the sanctimonious Christian woman. We bought that lie so we wanted no part of holiness. For years when I heard sermons on holiness, I closed my heart and ears. The moment the preacher said "holiness," I'd stare out the window or start counting the tiles in the ceiling. I didn't want to hear it. I thought, *If I've got to be like that ... well, maybe when I'm fifty....*

As long as I clung to that stereotype, I shut myself off to what God really wanted for me. But oh, how faithful our God is! He began to reveal Himself to me. He opened my mind, my heart and my eyes and began to teach me a true view of holiness. Once I finally understood what holiness really was, it became the pursuit of my life.

TRUE HOLINESS

To understand the true nature of holiness, you've got to understand the true nature of God. People often think God's chief attribute is love, but it is holiness. The Word tells us that the cherubim and seraphim around the throne of God say one thing, and they say it continually—every day, every moment of every day: "Holy, holy, holy, Lord God Almighty" (Revelation 4:8). They never stop extolling the holiness of God.

Once I discovered that holiness is God's chief attribute, His words in 1 Peter took on a personal meaning for me.

> He who called you is holy, you also be holy in all your conduct, because it is written, "Be holy, for I am holy" (1 Peter 1:15-16).

God is holy and He commands that we be holy also.

Our holy and beautiful God, the Creator of all that is magnificent and beautiful, the One who dwells in brilliant light on a sapphire throne, with a brightness around the throne like a rainbow described in *The Living Bible* in Ezekiel 1:22 as "inexpressibly beautiful," has a specific purpose for the women He created. He certainly did not create women to conform to the wrong concept I used to have or the backwards concept Hollywood pushes or any negative concept you might have of holiness. The behavior that "becomes holiness" is an inner quality of consecration to God that cannot help but produce an outer beauty.

The most beautiful women I've known have been those who walk in the deepest holiness. I remember when we first came to Calvary Chapel— the tiny little gathering on Church Street—I was a young pastor's wife in my thirties. God began bringing in a number of precious women, most in their sixties or older, who would come for our Thursday morning prayer meetings. What sweet, dear, godly, loving women they were! Every time I met with them in prayer, I was lifted up in the Lord. Watching them made me want to live a godlier, holier life. I wanted to grow to be like they were because the holiness of their lives inspired and touched me.

QUALITIES OF HOLINESS

A woman "whose behavior becomes holiness"—or reflects holiness—is a vibrant woman because she is continually filled to overflowing with the living water. When you meet a woman who is overflowing with the living water that Christ gives, you'll see a woman who was changed and transformed like the woman at the well (John 4). Remember what a mess she was? After she met Jesus and He gave her that living water, she went out to tell everybody about Him. Her influence was so strong that people came out to the well themselves to see who in the world this Man was, and how He could have such a powerful effect on this immoral woman.

The woman whose behavior reflects holiness is a radiant woman because she's infused with the light of Jesus Christ. His light dwells in her, and out of her comes that light. She doesn't have to make an effort to shine forth light. She doesn't think, *"I've got to be salt and light."* She just is. It's like a candle burning inside and its light simply emanates from her. She's the candleholder and the candle is Jesus Christ. He radiates through her.

The holy woman is peaceful because she has her mind stayed on Jesus. "You will keep him in perfect peace whose mind is stayed on You, because he trusts in You" (Isaiah 26:3). She's unflustered because she trusts God.

The holy woman is joyful. Since she walks in obedience, she doesn't have a lot of guilt to disturb her emotions. Sin is a joy robber. You can't have sin in your life and still have joy. But for the woman who walks in obedience, nothing can rob her of joy. Even when you go through very difficult circumstances, you can still have joy. You may not be happy, but you can still experience the living joy of a relationship with Jesus Christ, knowing He is with you even in those trials.

The holy woman is fruitful because she abides in Christ. John 15:5 says, "If we abide in Him and His words abide in us, we will bear much fruit." She is able to bear much fruit because she's an influencer. She brings Jesus with her into every situation and teaches something of Him wherever she goes.

The holy woman is satisfied because she hungers and thirsts after righteousness—and Jesus promised those who do this will be blessed and fulfilled. This woman never stops hungering and thirsting after Jesus. Just as the deer pants after the water brooks, so her soul pants after God continually (Psalm 42:1). She looks to Him for fulfillment. When she feels empty inside, she doesn't turn to the world. Instead, she turns to Him and says, "Lord, You promised You would satisfy me, so I look to You. Will You give me a Scripture today that will satisfy my longing heart?" And He does it. He answers her need and fulfills her innermost desire so she isn't hungering and searching after things that would displease God.

The holy woman is loving because she walks in prayerful communion with Jesus. She's not filled with bitterness, unforgiveness, malice or wrath. Instead, her words are peaceful, gentle and loving.

EXAMPLES OF HOLINESS

I've been so grateful for the gentle, patient, loving women God has brought to come alongside me over the years. In every church Chuck has pastored, I have been blessed by godly, older women who were like this—women who have had a strong influence on my life because they showed me Jesus. I think back to one of our very first churches in Arizona when Chuck and I were just twenty-one years old and newly married. I was pretty young in the Lord at that time and had a lot of funny ideas. I remember that despite my youth and my wrong ideas, there was an older woman in that church who helped me along. She used to just sit and talk with me—never condemning or critical, but always loving and patient.

This was during the time I had very negative thoughts about holiness. I already had my own wrong ideas about that, but they were fortified by the experience of some friends we had met. They were a darling couple and near to our own age. She told me about a time when she had been in a "holiness church" and had walked into a service one night wearing a gold belt. At the end of the service, she had gone down to the altar to pray, but afterward some of the women grabbed her and began to lecture her about what she was wearing. "You cannot be a Christian and wear a gold belt!" they insisted. The poor thing had only been a Christian for a couple of months. After I heard her story, I was more convinced than ever that I didn't want any part of *that* holiness.

At this time in my life, I remember I loved popular music. My parents had stopped walking with the Lord when I was a young teen, so I spent my teen years listening to whatever kind of music I liked. By the time Chuck and I had married, I'd only been walking with the Lord for about a year, and I didn't feel any conviction about my preference in music. We lived in the back of the church and I would turn my radio to the popular music station and I just loved it. There was a root beer stand in town that held a contest with the radio station. They'd have the station play a popular song on the radio and whoever called in and guessed the song correctly would get a free root beer. Well, I was always calling in and guessing the song! They would ask my name and I'd say, "Kay Smith," and it would be broadcast over the radio.

But that wasn't all. Another time, someone else had a contest where they offered a little diamond for the person who could name the song. I knew the song, I called in, and I won. They sent me my little diamond. Wasn't I a lovely witness in my community? Well, some people in our church heard me on the radio. I don't know how they heard, but they did. And they went to that dear, patient lady in our church and talked about it with her. She then came to me. I'll never forget her tenderness and love.

She didn't say, "Kay, you just can't listen to popular music. It isn't done. Don't you know better? Blah, blah, blah." Instead, she just lovingly said, "You know, somebody heard about you calling into the radio station and they just don't know what to think." She did it in such a sweet way that I didn't want to listen to popular music anymore.

I'll be honest—it was hard for me to give it up. I really loved it at the time. But God was beginning His work of holiness in my life. That kind of music didn't reflect my walk with Him. So He took it away. He used that sweet, loving, older woman to begin that work in me.

BEHAVIOR REFLECTING HOLINESS
When Jesus lives within you, His sweetness flows naturally out of you. But without Him, you're filled with only bitterness. I remember a few years back when Chuck and I ran into a woman we had known in one of our earlier churches. She was about seventy-five years old when we saw her and she was a very unhappy, belligerent woman. As we stood talking with her, we heard all about her life. She didn't like this and she didn't like that. She was mad at the world. She couldn't stand the convalescent home, and boy, she'd tear it down if she could! The longer she went on, the wider our eyes got. We weren't used to that kind of complaining.

When she walked away, Chuck said, "Whew!" and I said, "Feisty little thing, isn't she?" Then he said, "Just think what she would do if she weren't a Christian." Her behavior did not "reflect holiness." She didn't radiate Jesus' sweetness, tenderness or beauty.

The body of Christ needs women whose behavior is reverent—women who show consecration to Christ. What does it mean to be consecrated? It means being separated from the world—separated from the worldly system, worldly values, and worldly pleasures. It means having the love of the Father so evident in your heart that there's no room for the love of the world. It means being devoted to God and being set apart for Him. The woman who has consecrated herself to God is willing to be used by Him in any way He desires, but she won't let the world use her at all. She knows she's a child of God, and anyone watching her life can see that as well. She is an accurate representative of God and of Jesus Christ.

The people who influenced me the most towards Jesus were those whose conduct was godly. And again, lest you younger women think, *This doesn't mean me*, let me remind you that you are teaching and influencing lives too. You are either influencing lives toward God or away from Him.

I want to speak a specific word to young mothers. Please, let your behavior in the home reflect holiness and godliness. Remember that little eyes are watching you and little ears are taking in every word you say. Cease from the yelling and the screaming and the calling of names and all the things mothers are prone to do—things that are easy to do if you're not mindful of your influence. Ask God to give you a fresh infusion of His love and a glimpse of His holiness.

Second Peter 3:11 explains that since the world is in the process of being dissolved, we ought to be consecrated and holy in our behavior and be devout and godly in our lives. First Thessalonians 4:7 says, "God did not call us to uncleanness, but to holiness."

CHASTENING

No one likes chastening, but it is necessary. We need it. If we profess to be His children and we do not truly represent Him as we should or walk in holiness, we need to be chastened. Hebrews 12:10 says this:

> For [our earthly fathers] disciplined us for only a short period of time and chastised us as seemed proper and good to them; but He disciplines us for our certain good, that we may become sharers in His own holiness (*TLB*).

If you are a child of the living God and you do not willingly desire holiness, He will begin to discipline and chasten you so you will want to walk in holiness before Him. I'd much rather choose to walk in holiness than have to be disciplined into it. My mother used to say, "If you keep up that behavior, you are going to get a spanking!" Did your mother say that to you? The choice was yours. You could change your behavior or receive the discipline.

A lot of times we didn't change our behavior and we received what we needed. God sometimes has to do that with us if we do not willingly choose to walk in holiness. He admonishes us in Hebrews 12:14 to "Pursue peace with all people, and holiness, without which no one will see the Lord." Those are not my words, they're God's words. Without holiness no one will ever see the Lord. That holiness comes when we dwell in Him and He dwells in us. He will produce it in our lives.

THE DANGER OF SLANDER

Looking back on our passage in Titus 2, we see two specific areas Paul instructed Titus to address with the older women—two things he wanted to warn them against. The first has to do with slander. Holy women are not to be false accusers.

I remember a situation once where someone made a terrible accusation against a person I knew. I was really bothered by what I had heard and I thought, *Where did that come from? That's such a horrible thing for that person to say!*

At that moment the Lord reminded me of Revelation 12:10, which describes Satan as being the "accuser of the brethren." It suddenly dawned on me that whenever we falsely accuse another person, we become Satan's spokesperson. Isn't that a horrific thought? Now, I don't know about you, but I don't want to be Satan's mouthpiece.

Way back when I was a little girl in Sunday school, we used to sing,

> Be careful, little mouth, what you say,
> Be careful, little mouth, what you say,
> For the Father is up above
> and He's looking down in love,
> Be careful, little mouth, what you say. [4]

It's a good reminder. Be careful, little mouth, because slander and false accusations have destroyed people's reputations, their effectiveness and their influence. Sometimes it sidelines its victims.

Early in our marriage, I worked for an employer who was not a Christian. I tried really hard to witness to him about the Lord. He always listened but he never responded. Then one day he just said, "When I was sixteen years old I was very involved in a church. In fact, I used to help count the offering. One time a great deal of money went missing from the offering and the deacons sat me down and accused me of stealing the money. I didn't do it, and I told them I didn't, but they wouldn't listen to me. They brought the accusation straight to my parents." Then he said, "Kay, I've never set foot in a church again."

Do you see the pain slander can cause, and how utterly destructive it can be? Think about your own feelings when Satan accuses you. "You're pretty rotten, you know. Look at all the horrible things you've done." Your heart hears that and you get sick inside. Sometimes you even agree with him. "Yes. That's me. I'm rotten." That's a horrid feeling. God doesn't want us suffering in that way and He doesn't want us inflicting those feelings on anyone else.

If you have accused someone falsely, ask God for His forgiveness. And then go to the person you told this accusation to and make it right. Admit you spoke falsely. It's hard to do and our flesh hates it. But believe me, it will keep you from ever doing it again.

If the person you've slandered knows what you've done—if your words have come back around to that person—then you must go and make it right with them too. You must go and apologize for what you've done. But if the slander hasn't reached their ears, telling them will only hurt and grieve them.

I know about a situation where one man went to another and said, "You know, I didn't like you. And I told people that. I told them all about how awful I thought you were. But then when I really got to know you, I found out you weren't like that at all. I'm really sorry." It devastated the man who had been slandered. He was crushed to think he gave that impression to anybody. You can create more sorrow and heartache by sharing all that ugliness with the person. Don't do it.

BE FILLED WITH THE SPIRIT

The second warning Paul gave for the older women was not to be "given to much wine" (Titus 2:3). There's a good reason for this. Drinking much wine will not tend to godliness or behavior that reflects holiness.

Now, Chuck and I do not drink at all, and we wish nobody drank at all. That's my stand, although I certainly don't want to put myself in the place of judgment. The issue is between you and the Lord. But the Bible is very clear you're not to be given to much wine. Ephesians 5:18 gives us the alternative:

> And be not drunk with wine, wherein is excess, but be filled with the Spirit (KJV).

Be filled with the Spirit. Don't you love that? Don't you love when you ask the Holy Spirit to fill you, and He does? He anoints you and blesses you, and you feel completely revitalized by His presence and by the joy of walking with Him.

Unlike being filled with wine—which leads to debauchery and all manner of unpleasant, embarrassing behavior—being filled with the Spirit results in behavior that reflects holiness. You'll find yourself speaking out in psalms and hymns and spiritual songs.

Ephesians 5:19 reads,

> Speaking to one another in psalms and hymns and spiritual songs, singing and making melody in your heart to the Lord.

Do you ever walk around the house while you're dusting the furniture and start singing a favorite worship song? You can't help but feel the joy of the Lord when you do that. I remember times when I would be singing an old favorite like "Wait Upon the Lord" or "In His Time," and I'd get so carried away I'd think, *Oh, that'll be fun to play!* So before I could stop myself, I'd run over to the piano and start playing. Then I'd think, *Better get that dusting done!*

When we're filled with the Holy Spirit, the joy of the Lord feeds our spirit and lifts us out of the mundane. We can be doing something we previously considered such drudgery—like washing dishes—and suddenly it's not drudgery anymore. Suddenly it's an opportunity to enjoy spending time with Jesus. The suds are flying and we're filled with joy.

That's the kind of life He wants us to have—not the kind of life where we're staggering around the house with a hangover, awakening to the fact that we need to apologize to the neighborhood for our behavior the night before. What a glorious addiction to be addicted to the filling of the Holy Spirit instead!

TEACHERS OF GOOD

After those warnings, Paul told Titus to exhort the older women to be teachers of good things. Oh, how needed this reminder is! There's a terrible deficit in the world today because older women have not been teachers of good things, especially Christian women. Once the feminist movement started "raising consciousness," it left a wake of empty, unhappy, unfulfilled, frustrated, selfish, godless lives behind. It didn't work. Instead, it began destroying our nation, our families, our marriages, and our children.

In contrast to that kind of fruitless teaching, I've been blessed by the influence of several godly women. Some I've known personally, while others have influenced me through their writing. What these women had in common was living a life consecrated to God.

One of those women was a lady we all called Mother Mitchell. That godly, holy woman influenced me clear up to the very last time I saw her when she was in her nineties. I still remember her vibrancy and beauty in Christ.

I remember a time when she was introduced to a bunch of hippie kids at our Idyllwild camp. Those kids could spot phoniness in anybody, although I knew there wasn't a single phony thing about Mother Mitchell, I wasn't sure how they would relate to her. But godliness transcends generations and connects hearts. At that camp, those kids fell madly in love with Jesus and they fell madly in love with Mother Mitchell, through whom they saw Jesus. They wanted to sit at her feet and hear more and more. Doesn't that make you want to be a woman whose behavior reflects holiness?

Chuck's mom, Maude Elizabeth, was one of the greatest influences in my life. I never heard her say an unkind word about anybody. We lived in her home for about five months at the beginning of our marriage, and she lived with us for a time at the very end of her life, and I never saw Mom do an unkind deed.

She taught me how to bathe my first baby. She taught me to pray for my babies when they were sick. She taught me how to really get into the Word and to pray the first thing in the morning. She taught me how to love Jesus. I wish every mother-in-law could be like that.

CHOOSE THE HOLY PATH

You have a choice about the kind of woman you want to become. No one can make that choice for you. Which path do you desire? Proverbs 4:18 tells us, "The path of the just is like the shining sun, that shines ever brighter unto the perfect day."

One Sunday morning we were singing "When I Survey the Wondrous Cross," and as the words began to penetrate my heart, it occurred to me that if we would meditate on Jesus and on the great sacrifice He made in order to purchase us out of sin, it would give us all the motive we need to choose a godly, holy path. Think about the love of Jesus for you, dear sister. Ask Jesus to fill you with so much love for Him that you will desire holiness above anything else in your life.

> See, from His head, His hands, His feet,
> Sorrow and love flow mingled down;
> Did e're such love and sorrow meet,
> Or thorns compose so rich a crown?
>
> Were the whole realm of nature mine,
> That were a present far too small;
> Love so amazing, so divine,
> Demands my soul, my life, my all. [5]

Father, thank You for the work of Your Holy Spirit in our lives. May You fill us with the desire to please You and be like You. May we go forth as women whose behavior reflects Your holiness.

In Jesus' precious name. Amen.

CHAPTER

4

SHE SOWS
TO THE SPIRIT

HAVE YOU EVER NOTICED how often the Bible speaks about gardening? Start looking for that when you're reading through the Scriptures.
You'll find numerous references to gardens and vineyards, planters and
harvesters.

In John 15:1, depending on which version you are reading, God is
referred to as the vinedresser, husbandman, and the gardener. Song of
Solomon is filled with references to the garden. Psalm 1:3 tells us that
the one who delights in the laws of God will be like a tree planted by the
river. And of course, we can't forget the original garden we read about in
Genesis chapter 2.

Why the repetition of gardening as an illustration? I think God does that because all around us we're able to observe His laws in effect through nature. We plant something in the ground and after a time it grows. If we plant good seeds, good things grow. If we plant something disgusting—like turnips—then something bad grows. That's just a personal opinion, of course.

Galatians 6:7-9 gives some timeless truths about sowing and reaping:

> Do not be deceived, God is not mocked; for whatever a man sows, that he will also reap. For he who sows to his flesh will of the flesh reap corruption, but he who sows to the Spirit will of the Spirit reap everlasting life. And let us not grow weary while doing good, for in due season we shall reap if we do not lose heart.

Such a beautiful promise! I encourage you to read that over and over until it becomes a part of your thinking. Read it in other versions too. *The Living Bible* says it this way:

> Don't be misled. Remember that you can't ignore God and get away with it. A man will always reap just the kind of crop he sows. If he sows to please his own wrong desires, he will be planting seeds of evil and he will surely reap a harvest of spiritual decay and death. But if he plants the good things of the Spirit, he will reap the everlasting life which the Holy Spirit gives him. And let us not get tired of doing what is right, for after a while we will reap a harvest of blessing if we don't get discouraged and give up.

PLANTING SEEDS: GOOD OR BAD

I want you to hear this very clearly—we are planting seeds every single day. It's not optional. As Charles Spurgeon said, "It is not an open question at all whether I sow or not today." The question isn't open because there's only one answer to it—yes, you are sowing. He added, "The only question to be decided is: Shall I sow good seed or bad? Every man is always sowing." [6]

The truth is, you probably started planting seeds around breakfast time this morning. What was your attitude when you woke up and wandered into the kitchen? Did you feel thankful for another new day? Did you plant some seeds of praise and thanksgiving and prayer and a little bit of intercession? Or did you get out of bed in a grouchy mood and make everybody else feel grouchy too? The sowing starts when your feet hit the floor and it continues throughout the day. You plant seeds with everyone you come in contact with. You plant seeds in your own mind by what you read and what you watch on TV.

We are living in an age when we don't have to look far at all to find bad seed. I cannot believe the vulgarity permitted on TV. I really can't. You can turn on almost any program and find it filled with all kinds of sexual references. It's just absolute pollution. Satan knows that by appealing to this particular side of people's lives, he is able to capture them, lead them down the wrong path, and then ultimately destroy them. Beloved sister, you must be on guard against this.

This might startle you, but I have frequently asked God to curse the vulgar things I've seen in my area. There was once a vile business down on Newport Boulevard with an awful picture on the side of the wall that was clearly visible when I drove by. Unfortunately, I drove by a lot. So I began to pray God would curse that picture. My husband and my sons drove down Newport Boulevard! I didn't want them to have to see that. Well, it didn't take long. Before I knew it, the place was empty and the awful picture was gone too. I went by and could see through the open front door that the place was completely deserted. God is so great.

Another time there was a dance place down on Harbor Boulevard called Baby Dolls. Same thing—vile pictures, vile activity. A friend and I found ourselves on that road together frequently, and every time we went by, we'd just say, "God, we curse that place in the name of Jesus." Sure enough, the business went under and the owner left town. Before he moved away, he gave an interview to the paper in which he stated he had never had such a struggle in business in all his life.

I pray some of you reading this feel God's calling to take that kind of firm stand. Through your prayers, ask God to destroy such vulgarity. You can be sure that when you pray along those lines, you are praying the will of God. Satan is constantly throwing bad seed in front of us. We should pray for God to destroy that seed. Sometimes I'm concerned at the passivity in the Christian church. We have the power of God through prayer. Let's use it!

WHAT YOU SOW IS WHAT YOU REAP

I once read an interview with Malcolm Muggeridge in *Christianity Today*. As I've stated before, Malcolm Muggeridge had a brilliant mind. He had been through an interesting journey on his way to Christ. For most of his life he was a socialist and then he became a humanist. It wasn't until the sunset years of his life, as he described it, that he accepted Jesus. He would sometimes say one of his ministries was to set people straight in their thinking about spiritual things.

In this particular article, the interviewer asked him about the significance of marriage in our modern society. Malcolm began to share his thoughts about marriage and its importance, and then spoke about the foolishness of people who ignore marriage and choose simply to live together. Asked why it was foolish, he said this simple sentence that stayed with me long after I finished reading the article. He said, "God is not mocked." [7]

I think most of us have dealt with this situation. We know people who have chosen to live together without marriage. And if you're like me, you try to think up good answers to their arguments about why that little piece of paper is not important. I've had all those discussions in the past.

I'd say, "Well, the deed to our house is just a little piece of paper, but think what it represents." Or I'd use money as an example. "It's also just a piece of paper, but it represents so much more." But I was never really satisfied with those answers. Then I read Malcolm Muggeridge's answer: "God is not mocked." That's it. That's the answer to why it is foolishness to live together apart from marriage: God will not be mocked.

When you violate God's laws, you will reap the consequences. It may not happen today or tomorrow or next month, but it will happen eventually. God has set certain laws in motion and that is just the way it is. You see it every day. You plant, you harvest. You sow, you reap. There will definitely come a time of reaping.

People would say to Malcolm Muggeridge, "Oh, you have such insight into the future. You're kind of a prophet." But he would answer, "I'm not a prophet. I'm just a man who points out consequences." We need people today who are willing to point out the consequences. "If you do this, this will be the result." When you think about it, that is one of the roles of a prophet. Jeremiah told the children of Israel again and again, "If you do not turn and repent, you will go into captivity" (Jeremiah 29:14). And that's exactly what happened. Oh, how the church needs its prophets!

The church needs prophets, but it also needs teachers who are willing to point out the consequences of disobedience. I cannot tell you the number of times I've tried to counsel Christian women in their thirties—women who certainly should know better—who have gotten themselves involved with married men. In every situation, God has led me to point out that they would eventually reap the consequences of their choices through their children.

Women often talk themselves into such a sin by telling themselves, "I can handle the consequences of this myself." But we aren't just hurting ourselves when we disobey. Time and again, I've watched what these choices have done to children. What a woman indulges in herself, she will grieve over in her children. Let that be a warning to you. There's not a passion in this world that's worth sacrificing your children for.

SIN DECEIVES

Sin is deceitful. Keep that in mind. "Do not be deceived," God warns us in Galatians 6:7, and elaborates on it in Hebrews 3:13 saying, "Exhort one another daily ... lest any of you be hardened through the deceitfulness of sin." Satan is a liar. He doesn't come charging at you with a pitchfork. He sneaks in. "This is the way to happiness," he says in his subtle, deceitful tone.

Like Eve, we can be foolish enough to entertain those thoughts. Then, because those lies are so appealing, we opt to believe them instead of the words of God. Have you ever given thought to how easy it is to take Eve's road? Allegra Harrah, my friend and author of the book, *Prayer Weapons*, once said, "All of us have just enough Eve in us to believe Satan at times." [8] He deceived Eve and he continues to deceive women today.

Teenage drivers are not accident-prone because of a lack of skill in driving. They are accident-prone because of faulty judgment. They simply do not look ahead and see the consequences of their misbehavior. They think they can pass a car and they don't stop to question whether another car might be coming toward them. They're going to hit head-on or they're going to run somebody off the sidewalk. You may have seen teenage boys turn a corner on two wheels and just miss a child or barely avoid a horrible collision.

But teenagers are not the only people who think—mistakenly—that they can get away with doing whatever they want to do. Sin deceives. Consequences will happen, because God is not mocked. To mock means literally to "turn up your nose in scorn." So when we mock God, we are mocking His Word. We are turning up our noses at the laws He has given us. We are holding His commandments in contempt.

Doesn't that sound awful? And it is! To scorn the Word of God is a shameful, horrible thing. Yet this is what we do when we go our own way, when we choose what feels good over what we know to be right. If you commit adultery because it seems pleasurable to you, if you bear false witness, if you covet what belongs to someone else—you will reap consequences eventually. This is not to say you can't be forgiven of your sins. You can.

First John 1:9 promises, "If we confess our sins, He is faithful and just to forgive us our sins and to cleanse us from all unrighteousness." But the truth is, forgiveness does not always eliminate the natural consequences of our sin. You can be forgiven of an adulterous affair but you can still reap the consequences through your children or through the destruction of your marriage or the loss of your reputation or ministry.

PLANTING IN YOUR MIND

I doubt very much that most people set out to purposely destroy their lives. I really don't believe it happens that way. I think what happens is that people are not selective about the things they allow their minds to dwell on. Everything you plant in your mind will bear fruit—everything.

That's why it's so important to have discretion about the kinds of things you allow into your mind. If you sit around having ungodly, gossipy conversations with your friends and you don't do one thing to get out of that conversation, or to repent and ask God to remove it from you, you're going to reap from that conversation.

Words are going to come to your mind and you'll think, *Why in the world do I feel like saying those words?* It's because you've subjected your mind to those words in ungodly conversations and you haven't asked God to uproot those seeds.

What you put into your mind will come out in your words and actions. I think one of the worst things you can allow into your mind is discontentment. That's a bad seed if ever I saw one. Too many women, and Christian women at that, fall into this trap. "I'm not happy in my marriage," they'll say. Say that to yourself enough times and eventually you'll start saying, "I have got to get out of my marriage."

I knew a woman once who went from allowing discontentment into her mind to voicing that discontentment to eventually divorcing her husband. Later she said, "You know, I thought I was doing the right thing at the time but I've always been sorry." Then she said, "I reaped through my children. Not one of my children knows the Lord." The children suffered the most from her decision. As I said before, forgiveness will always be available to you, but that doesn't mean your choice won't leave a lot of scars and sadness.

Charles "Tex" Watson is a powerful example of this. If you remember, he was a member of the Manson Family that took part in the murder of seven people in 1969. He was arrested, convicted, and sentenced to death, although his sentence was later reduced to a life sentence. Early in his incarceration, Charles gave his life to Christ and began, what is still today, a thriving prison ministry called Abounding Love Ministries. Currently, Charles is an ordained minister … but he is still in prison. Although he's been forgiven of his crimes, he is still reaping the consequences of his horrible actions all those years ago.

Because God doesn't rain down fire on us the moment we choose to sin, people often think they're getting away with it. They think God doesn't notice. But you know what God is doing? He isn't up there plotting for the time when He'll rain down fire. He's grieving, because He loves even those who are disobeying, and He knows that by their sin they've put the law of sowing and reaping into motion.

SOWING TO THE FLESH

"For he who sows to his flesh will of the flesh reap corruption" (Galatians 6:8). The *Amplified Bible* elaborates on this:

> For he who sows to his own flesh, his lower nature and sensuality, will from the flesh reap decay and ruin and destruction.

Isn't that a vivid warning? So what is sowing to the flesh? Paul gave us a list of the works of the flesh:

> Now the works of the flesh are evident, which are: adultery, fornication, uncleanness, lewdness, idolatry, sorcery, hatred, contentions, jealousies, outbursts of wrath, selfish ambitions, dissensions, heresies, envy, murders, drunkenness, revelries, and the like (Galatians 5:19-21).

That's a pretty awful list of the works of the flesh—but what is the flesh? It's the life we lead as though God didn't exist. The one who lives completely wrapped up in his or her own selfish desires with a complete disregard for everyone else is the one who is living in the flesh. Put more clearly, that's the one who is being ruled by the flesh. When the flesh rules you, you walk in deliberate defiance and disobedience to God's will.

Paul goes on to say,

> Those who practice such things will not inherit the kingdom of God (Galatians 5:21).

The thought of that just makes my heart ache. It hurts me to think of those people I know who are practicing these works of the flesh and who do not yet know Jesus. I pray they turn to Him and repent before it is too late.

Now, if you do belong to Jesus and you are indulging in any of these works of the flesh—even something like hatred or discord or wrath— you can be sure chastening will come into your life at some point. God chastens those He loves (Hebrews 12:6), not to punish but to redirect you and prepare you for heaven.

This is such a serious thing that I want you to take a moment right now to read that list again and bring each one before the Lord. Ask Him, "Lord, am I indulging in this work of the flesh? Am I mocking You in any of these things?" If you do feel conviction over any of them, ask God to root them out.

SOWING TO THE SPIRIT

Those are the bad seeds. Here are the good seeds. And I'm so glad to get past the works of the flesh and focus on the works of the Spirit!

> But he who sows to the Spirit will of the Spirit reap everlasting life (Galatians 6:8).

How do we sow to the Spirit? There are dozens of ways. We sow to the Spirit in our actions and in our attitudes. We can sow to the Spirit, for instance, by having a thankful attitude instead of a complaining attitude. The more often we choose thankfulness over complaining, the more that habit will be ingrained in us. Instead of being ruled by our flesh, we transfer control to the Holy Spirit. We become obedient. He fills us to overflowing with His joy and we find that we love as we ought to love. We look for opportunities to encourage others.

Years ago a friend from another church asked how I felt about the baptism of the Holy Spirit. I shared with her very openly. Her response was, "Well, that's nice. I see what you believe and that's fine for you, but it's not for me." I remember thinking, *Lord, why did I spend this whole afternoon on this? I could have been doing a million other things.*

But just as quickly as I had that thought, the Lord said, "Kay, you planted a seed and it will bear fruit. Don't try to make it grow. Just leave it alone." Twelve years later my friend received the baptism of the Holy Spirit. She told me, "You know, from the day you and I talked about it all those years ago, I have not been able to get away from it." Isn't that precious? So you're planting seeds.

God knows exactly how to bring a harvest out of the seeds we plant. When you take a moment to pray with your children before they leave for school, or when you speak some encouragement to a roommate or a neighbor, God knows just how to cultivate the soil of those hearts and cause those seeds to grow. You may feel what you're saying is pointless or without value, but it's not. God will bring about the harvest.

> And let us not grow weary while doing good, for in due season we shall reap if we do not lose heart (Galatians 6:9).

Do not lose heart. Keep doing that which you know to be right and good. Don't compromise.

WAITING FOR THE HARVEST

I often think of this verse when I'm counseling a single girl who is struggling with the desire to be married. I know it must be difficult to walk through this dark, wicked world without a partner. But it's so hard for me to see these beautiful Christian girls slowly begin to compromise. They start out walking with Jesus in very close fellowship, but then slowly, slowly, as time goes by and God doesn't bring them that bridegroom they're longing for, they begin to compromise and date unbelievers. I've watched some of them—against all our better counsel—enter into marriage with these unbelievers, have a child or two, and then go through a painful divorce. Many of these women have come back to me and shared, "Why didn't I wait on the Lord?"

Please take this to heart. Do not grow weary while doing good—persevere! If you're single and God hasn't brought that person along yet, don't try to rush Him. Don't push. And don't compromise. You are very special to God and He has a purpose for all you go through.

Some harvests won't be seen until we stand before the Lord. Many things won't be fulfilled here on earth but will have their completion in heaven. But sometimes we do get to see a seed come to full fruition.

Many years back, a friend of mine went through a painful divorce. She did not want her marriage to end. It was her husband's decision and it came after many years of marriage. She was broken-hearted, but she chose God's path of forgiveness and resisted the temptation of becoming bitter and resentful.

This wasn't easy, especially when her husband remarried. But she continued to walk in forgiveness and love. Every so often, he would call her just to talk. He had once accepted the Lord, but had walked far, far away from Him. She prayed for him and she let God's love flow from her heart to his. I don't want to make it sound like this was easy for her, because it wasn't. At times she felt hurt and vengeful, but when those feelings rose up, she refused to let them find lodging in her heart. She just kept praying for him.

After many years of this, her ex-husband became very sick and asked to see her. He was actually on his deathbed when she saw him. His new wife stayed in the room while they had their visit. My friend's ex-husband reached over, took her hand and he said, "I've never stopped loving you. Never! I saw Jesus in you. And I'm sorry for all the hurt I've brought you. I was selfish." There on his deathbed, my friend was able to lead her ex-husband back to Christ.

Every seed my friend had sown through her prayers was harvested in that room. She reaped something very sweet here on earth, and she will reap for eternity the life she helped to bring back to God.

A PROMISED HARVEST

A beautiful promise can be found in the words of the psalmist who said, "Those who sow in tears shall reap in joy" (Psalm 126:5). Are you discouraged with your sowing today? Have you been sowing in tears? Does it seem everyone else around you is leading a happy, trouble-free life, and you're the only one grieving and hurting? Take heart, beloved. Jesus sees every single tear you shed, and He promises that you will one day reap in joy.

But there's more. Psalm 126:6 goes on to say,

> He who continually goes forth weeping, bearing seed for sowing, shall doubtless come again with rejoicing, bringing his sheaves with him.

Isn't that beautiful? Keep that promise in mind as you go forth. Bring that precious seed with you and sow it wherever you go. Drop those seeds everywhere—seeds about Jesus, seeds of praise, seeds of joy and seeds of encouragement. Because if you go forth weeping, bearing precious seed, without a question of a doubt, you will come again with rejoicing. Can't you just picture the woman who planted all this wheat? And now her arms are just laden with all these sheaves of wheat she has gathered from her planting. That can be you.

Lord, by Your Holy Spirit, we ask that You give us more seed to plant. Oh, how we desire it. We want to plant Your seed in the lives of all we meet, and we want to plant Your seed in our own minds. Protect us, Lord. Keep us from the deceitfulness of sin. Make us love Your law. Cause us to plant only those things that will edify, only those things that will help us to walk in Your Spirit.

In Jesus' name we ask. Amen.

CHAPTER
5

SHE CONTINUALLY GROWS

Every wise woman buildeth her house: but the foolish plucketh it down with her hands (Proverbs 14:1 KJV).

I GET VERY AGGRAVATED WITH my plants in the house if I look at them and find there isn't any new growth. Unless it's their dormant season, a lack of new growth means something is wrong with them. It's exactly the same in our Christian life. We should always be growing and maturing in the Lord. If we're not—if there's no sign of new growth in us—it means we've allowed ourselves to become dormant.

Many things can cause that state of dormancy. Trials can do it. Sometimes grief can be so thick it puts us in a place of darkness where no light can get in. Laziness can do it too. If you allow yourself to just kick back long enough, you can stop the growth of any new leaves. The normal, every-day cares of this world can choke out new growth. Weeds of worry can overshadow the good things and keep you from growing as you ought.

Neglect can do it too. We can fill our lives with all kinds of fun activities, but fail to find time to sit at the feet of Jesus and talk to Him and learn from Him. It shouldn't surprise us then when we find we're not growing in the things of the Lord.

When we speak of growing spiritually, what does that mean? We can define growth as "springing up to maturity." That sounds so instanta-neous, doesn't it? I wish it could be like that, but it simply isn't. Christian maturity is a slow process. Growth takes time because growing in Christ means becoming Christlike—in our actions, reactions, attitudes, and our choices. We don't just arrive at that place overnight.

We've all heard the expression, "Oh, grow up!" That's something we tend to say (or think) when someone is behaving badly. In our minds we have a picture of what a grown-up, adult person ought to be. We expect cer-tain things out of them. They ought to have self-control and a quietness of spirit. They shouldn't behave like a toddler.

CHRISTIAN MATURITY

Just as we expect a certain level of maturity for adults, we expect Christians to reach a certain level of maturity as well. Paul, under the inspiration of the Holy Spirit, talked about it in Ephesians 4:14-15.

> We should no longer be children, tossed to and fro and carried about with every wind of doctrine, by the trickery of men, in the cunning crafti-ness of deceitful plotting, but, speaking the truth in love, may grow up in all things into Him who is the head—Christ.

If we belong to Jesus, our lives should not be characterized by instability or immaturity. Our lives should be on a continual path of growth until that day God causes us to look like Jesus. That work will continue right up until the day we see Him face to face. But for now, every day we live on this earth, we should be growing to be like Jesus.

Jesus said, "Be perfect, therefore, as your heavenly Father is perfect" (Matthew 5:48 *NIV*). "Perfect" in this instance means "of complete age"—not a chronological age. It means maturity. Jesus is not saying we must reach a state of sinless perfection. That's impossible while we're here on earth. He's talking about maturity, the kind you see when fruit on a tree has reached its peak of flavor and sweetness. The *Amplified Bible* gives us a beautiful description of this kind of maturity.

> Be ye perfect as your Father in heaven is perfect, that is, grow into complete maturity of godliness in mind and character (Matthew 5:48).

The behavior of the Corinthian church was so immature that Paul actually called them babies. They were characterized by envy, strife, division and immorality. They were Christians in the crib (1 Corinthians 3:1-3). We're all born into the kingdom as brand-new babies in the Lord. Babies are beautiful, but they're also self-centered and dependent.

One of my granddaughters, Caitlyn, used to love to put key rings in her mouth. Any time she got hold of one, in her mouth it went. But you know how filthy key rings are—especially leather ones. Everybody's handled them and they're just loaded with germs. And if they are made with any kind of dye, you just know that's coming off in the baby's mouth, and that can't be healthy. So Caitlyn's mama would always take the keys away from her. Of course, that would make Caitlyn scream and carry on.

Well, some Christians are like that. Let the Lord take some little toy away from her, and oh, you can hear her screaming from clear down the road.

She just can't stand to be told no. That's because she has never grown up in Jesus.

Proverbs 29:15 tells us, "A child left to himself brings shame to his mother." And an adult Christian who doesn't grow brings shame to the body of Christ. When people know you're a Christian but they see that you are immature in your faith, having all the same attitudes, actions and reactions as they do, the world doesn't see anything in your life that makes them thirsty for Jesus.

Just as good parents discipline their children in order to direct their behavior, so too, God disciplines the ones He loves. Through His love and discipline we grow—if we choose to. It's always a choice. You don't have to grow. It's your reaction to God's love and to God's discipline that determines whether or not you will grow.

SPIRITUAL BABIES

Did you know it's possible to be born again and yet remain a spiritual baby? Most of us know a few such babies who throw tantrums, exhibit envy, cause division and bring disgrace to the body of Christ. These are the ones who seem in perpetual need of pampering and coddling. They're completely dependent on others for spiritual food and counsel.

Now, it's wise to seek godly counsel when you're facing a hard decision. But I'm talking about people who can't seem to make any decisions for themselves at all without checking with someone else. Instead of going to God they go to another person. But we have Jesus Himself to be our counselor. Isaiah said His name would be Wonderful, Counselor (Isaiah 9:6). We also have the Holy Spirit to guide, teach and counsel us (John 14:26, 1 Corinthians 2:13). If you're one who feels you have to seek out someone else's advice before you make a move, I urge you to learn to go to the greatest Counselor there is, the One who can never fail you.

The dangerous thing about baby Christians is that they're unstable. Every time a new doctrine comes along, they chase after it. Not only does this cause confusion, it also wastes valuable time. So often we've had people run after some new doctrine, only to come back years later wanting Chuck to fix everything and complaining to him about all the time they threw away. If they had just stayed and grown through the faithful, consistent teaching of the Word, they could have matured to the point where they had enough discernment to see through a new, kooky doctrine.

Baby Christians don't learn humility. They never learn to walk in love and lowliness of mind. Instead, they're kind of prideful. They don't work at being peaceful with others and they don't bear the burdens of others. To me, that's one of the clearest indicators of immaturity—not being willing or able to bear someone else's burden. That comes from self-centeredness. Those who are focused on themselves don't have empathy for another.

Take stock of yourself. Are you growing today? If you can't say yes to that, then something needs to change. If for no other reason, we should want to grow because God's Word tells us to. God tells us to grow in grace, to grow in knowledge, to grow in love. He tells us to be mature.

The more mature you are in Christ, the better witness you will be to the world. A mature Christian woman suffers wrongs done against her and loves when she has every right to hate. The world is always shocked to see that. And that's exactly the kind of maturity Jesus wants to develop in us.

Maturity doesn't necessarily come with age. I have found that the older women I know who have walked with Jesus consistently through the years, growing continually in Him, have greater joy, greater peace and greater fulfillment than women their age who do not know Jesus.

When I became middle-aged, I discovered some fantastic things about growing older I hadn't expected to enjoy so much. I found out the things that were so important to me when I was twenty suddenly weren't important anymore. When I was in my thirties and I first noticed the crow's feet and the wrinkles starting to appear on my face, it bothered me. So I used all the masks and face creams that came along. But when I hit middle age, I stopped being bothered. I realized that wrinkles are inevitable. What are you going to do? I thought, *They're here, and they're here to stay.* So I stopped worrying. And that was a blessing!

You know, the first wrinkle is like the first dent on your new car. It's the worst one of all. After that, it doesn't matter so much—unless you let it. That's where maturity in Christ gives you the peace to accept what is. We know this is just a tent and we will be given a new, glorious body in heaven. But the worldly, older woman who doesn't have eternal hope, security or peace in Jesus doesn't always age with grace or dignity.

I have loved so many things about aging. Growing older has changed my priority list dramatically. After you've gone through enough sorrow and heartache yourself, and you've been a companion to others who have gone through their own loss and pain, all those small things that used to consume your thoughts and your energy just fade away.

God gives you a whole new list of priorities. Thoughts about who you are and where you are and whom you're with and how you're dressed—all that unimportant stuff loses the hold it once had. You suddenly discover pleasing Jesus has become the most important thing in the world.

Believe me, nothing else will ever be as fulfilling to you. You'll be filled with a peace and a joy that is untouchable. Your world won't come crashing down if a toy is taken away, or your plans don't work out the way you wanted. You have the maturity, the grace and the peace to accept it and just keep walking with Jesus.

WHAT HELPS US GROW?

So, what helps us grow? Well, we're not too different from plants in this respect. If you like to garden, you know plants must have good soil, air, light and water if they're to survive and develop. Without that combination, you won't have success with your plants. Christians have those same needs.

First, we need good soil so our roots will grow down deep. Psalm 92:13 tells us, "Those who are planted in the house of the LORD shall flourish in the courts of our God." What better soil could you ask for than to be planted in the house of the Lord? Ephesians 3:17 says we are to be "rooted and grounded in love." When we're firmly planted in the right soil, we can take root as we ought.

THE HEAVENLIES

Secondly, we need air. Spiritually speaking, air speaks of atmosphere. What kind of atmosphere is conducive to Christian growth? Well, we must first come to a realization of a few facts. Ephesians 2:6 says that we are seated in the heavenly places with Christ Jesus. We may not feel like that, but it's true. If you belong to God, then you are seated in the heavenlies with Jesus. He Himself told us, "Lo, I am with you always, even to the end of the age" (Matthew 28:20). So Jesus is with you now. He's with you wherever you go. That means you are dwelling in His atmosphere, in His presence. The key for us is to become aware of this.

Years ago, Ethel Waters used to sing at Billy Graham's crusades, and I remember her singing,

> If Jesus goes with me, I'll go anywhere!
> 'Tis Heaven to me, where'er I may be, if He is there!
> I count it a privilege here, His cross to bear,
> If Jesus goes with me, I'll go anywhere! [9]

Is that true for you? When you become aware of His constant presence with you, it won't matter how dark or shoddy your circumstances—you'll think, *Where Jesus is, 'tis heaven to me.*

Another atmospheric place that is so vital to our growth is church. It's the assembling together of God's family. Hebrews 10:24-25 reads,

> And let us consider one another in order to stir up love and good works, not forsaking the assembling of ourselves together.

What happens when you come to church in a bad mood or feeling a little depressed and suddenly you're around all these happy Christians? Your spirit is lifted. You hear the whole congregation worshiping together, singing words that remind you of God's constant, unchanging love for you, and you think, *Hey, I'm not forsaken. He loves me still.* By the time you leave, you're built back up again.

The God who created you knew that you needed this togetherness. He knew there would be times when you need the encouragement of other believers who have gone through the same trials you're facing. He knew that you needed to sit side-by-side with other people who love Jesus, lift your voices together, pore over the Word together, and be built up in the things of the Lord. And so He instructs us to "not forsake the assembling of ourselves together."

Not only are we to make sure we seek out the proper atmosphere, we're also told to avoid the wrong kind of atmosphere. Ephesians 5:11 admonishes, "Have no fellowship with the unfruitful works of darkness, but rather expose them." Christians err when they think they can fellowship with darkness and it won't affect them. It will. As we discussed in our last chapter, whatever seeds you allow to be sown in your mind are the seeds that will grow. If you're with people who are planting bad seeds, then bad seeds will grow in your heart and mind.

THE LIGHT OF JESUS

This brings us to our third need, which is light. What is our source of light? It is Jesus Himself. As He said in John 8:12,

> I am the light of the world. He who follows Me shall not walk in darkness, but have the light of life.

Jesus is the light, and His Word is a light to us.

> Your word is a lamp to my feet and a light to my path … The entrance of Your words gives light; it gives understanding to the simple (Psalm 119:105, 130).

Light is so important to our physical growth. Sunlight provides vitamin D, which our bodies need. I don't think mothers do this anymore, but when I had my babies, we were told to take our babies (who were to be wearing absolutely nothing) outside for "sun baths" for ten minutes each day—five on the tummy and five on the back. We did this to avoid rickets, which is softening of the bones, caused by a lack of vitamin D.

We also put our children out to play. Every day. Right after breakfast, and after they brushed their teeth, we sent them out to play, and they stayed outside till lunchtime. And, oh, the fun they had! They built forts and towed their wagons around the block. They had neighborhood fairs and lemonade stands, and sometimes they jumped off the garage roof which made me frantic. But they were healthy, tan little kids.

There's such a fear of the sun these days. I know we have to be careful to avoid overexposure, but we shouldn't do away with it completely. Our need for vitamin D hasn't gone away. I think everyone needs to get out in the fresh air and sunshine for at least a little while every day. There's something about sunlight that relaxes us. It has a calming effect on the body. And if it's so good for us physically, how much more beneficial is it to us spiritually?

Have you ever been in a very dark restaurant and noticed all the beautiful plants they have hanging everywhere? There's one such restaurant in Orange County where Chuck and I like to go for dinner. I used to look up at those plants and think, *How in the world can they keep such gorgeous plants in this dark restaurant?*

But then I learned what they do. They hire a plant service, which brings in those beautiful Boston ferns and places them in all the dark, dingy corners. They leave them hanging there in the darkness until those poor little plants can't stand the lightless atmosphere anymore and start drooping and turning brown and looking awful. Then they take those plants out and they replace them.

You know, Satan loves to do that with Christians. He runs a really hideous plant service. He likes to find a Christian who is walking closely with Jesus and he tries to lure her away to some dark corner where she absolutely can't grow. Then, when the darkness has done its work and the poor plant is all drooped and withered and showing the effects of no light and no air, he decides you're of no use to him anymore. The damage is done.

This is what happens when we follow the path Satan lays out before us. Don't get caught in dark places. Don't think you can linger there long and not feel the effects. Stay in the light of Jesus.

THE LIVING WATER

Lastly, we have a great need for water. How necessary it is to life! You can go without food a long time, but you can't last long without water. Not only is it vital for inner nourishment, but we also need it outwardly to cleanse and refresh us.

In that way, we're not unlike a plant. Leaves must be washed, because an accumulation of dust can hinder the intake of carbon dioxide and sunlight. If that happens, they won't produce enough chlorophyll to stimulate growth. Dusty plants don't grow as they should. Well, if we want to grow, we need to be cleansed too.

We need the cleansing of God's Word. In speaking of the great sacrifice Jesus gave out of His love for the church, Paul said in Ephesians 5:26, "That He might sanctify and cleanse her with the washing of water by the word."

The Bible tells us that Jesus offers us His living water, and it alone can satisfy our thirst.

> Jesus answered and said to her, "Whoever drinks of this water will thirst again, but whoever drinks of the water that I shall give him will never thirst. But the water that I shall give him will become in him a fountain of water springing up into everlasting life" (John 4:13-14).

Thirst is a blessing if it causes you to run to Jesus. He has promised that those who hunger and thirst after righteousness shall be filled (Matthew 5:6). Isn't that a precious promise? When your thirst for Him sends you to the Word or sends you to prayer, you can be confident the Holy Spirit will fill you up and satisfy that longing.

The Piggyback plant is a very durable, very tolerant houseplant. But if you've ever seen one that's been deprived too long of water, you know it's about the droopiest plant ever. It just looks horrible with those sad, wilted leaves. But if you water it and then wait about an hour, all of a sudden it's perked up and beautiful again.

If we don't have the living water that Jesus offers abiding and overflowing in us, we can become like those droopy little Piggybacks. And it shows. We may think nobody can see, but people know. When you're a well-watered garden, that shows too.

So we need it all—good soil, air, light and water. If we have those things, we will most certainly grow. When we're rooted in His love, strengthened by the knowledge of His constant presence, bathed in His light, and nourished by His living water, we can face whatever comes with an assurance that He's working something out for our own good and growth. This is so vital! If you don't face adversity with faith, you'll face it with bitterness.

GROWTH THROUGH TRIALS

I have found that those who aren't aware of the purpose of suffering often stop growing when adversity comes. We have to greet trials with faith. No one likes emotional or physical pain, but we have to remember God's purpose is to grow us up to look and act like Jesus, and He can and will bring whatever means He finds necessary to accomplish that purpose.

Whenever I think of the growth that comes through trials, Corrie ten Boom comes to mind. You have to wonder how different the outcome would have been if she had turned bitter toward God in that prison, if she had let the fleas and the cruel guards and the loss of her father and sister turn her heart against God. She could have said, "God, I have served You all my life—and this is what You've brought me to? I give up." But she didn't. Instead, she said, "Teach me how to live in this place, Lord. Teach me how to live."

Because of that, God gave Corrie a ministry that spread far and wide. She traveled all over the world sharing her story with others. She shared it in person, on the radio, and in the many books she has written, translated into numerous languages. She even managed to get into prisons where men couldn't go. She'd talk to those prisoners and tell them, "I was behind bars once, just like you." They'd stare at that benign-looking, lovely, sweet elderly lady with bewilderment—but they could relate to her. They knew she understood them.

All of that would have been lost if Corrie had not accepted the suffering that came her way. When we know the Lord and we trust His ways, beautiful things can come from the harshest of circumstances.

An even closer example, for me personally, was Chuck's mom. As I've said again and again, she was probably the godliest woman I have ever met. It was she who taught me to raise my babies in faith.

When Dad and Bill Smith were killed in a plane crash, I watched how she reacted. She could have gotten bitter. Bill was her youngest son, and only twenty-four years old. She could have said, "Lord, I've raised all my children to know You. Every one of them is walking with You and they all love You. I taught them to live by faith. I read to them and prayed for them and did everything You required of me. And now You've taken my husband and son? That's it."

She could have turned her face from God, but instead she looked up and said, "God, You know what is best." She kept loving Jesus. In fact, she loved Him all the more, and she walked with Him until the day she died. Just a few days before she passed away, despite tremendous suffering due to her cancer and despite knowing she was dying, I watched her raise her hands to Jesus and praise Him.

I can't help but wonder where my husband might be if Mom Smith had turned bitter toward God instead of accepting what He permitted to come her way. I wonder if Chuck would have continued walking with the Lord or if he would have become a pastor. I wonder if Calvary Chapel would have even come into being if Mom had refused to go through the suffering that God wanted her to bear.

As Paul said so well,

> I beseech you therefore, brethren, by the mercies of God, that you present your bodies a living sacrifice, holy, acceptable to God, which is your reasonable service (Romans 12:1).

If you're going through suffering today, accept it as a tool God has allowed for your growth. Not only will you grow, but you'll also gain comfort you can pass on to others when they need it. Let God grow you up. Allow Him to bring whatever is necessary so you may be mature and complete.

It's a blessed place to be, as the old hymn, "Higher Ground," so sweetly tells us.

> My heart has no desire to stay
> Where doubts arise and fears dismay;
> Though some may dwell where those abound
> My prayer, my aim
> Is higher ground. [10]

Let's ask Him to take us to higher ground.

Father, make Your Word real to our hearts. I ask for Your Holy Spirit to touch the heart of every woman reading this, that He would put in each heart a renewed desire to walk with You in a more steadfast way than she's ever walked before. Grow us up, Lord—no matter what it takes. Make us to look like Jesus and act like Jesus, that the watching world will see Him reflected in us, and will reach for the hope He offers.

We ask our requests in Jesus' name. Amen.

CHAPTER

6

SHE IS JOYFUL IN TRIALS

WHEN OUR GRANDSON, WILLIAM, was about two-and-a-half, his mother saw he was doing something that needed correction. "William," she said, "I don't like your attitude."

Right back at her, with a look that said he was very tired of that subject, he said, "Attitude, attitude, attitude."

Your attitude can really make a difference, can't it? An attitude can be described as a feeling about a person or a thing. And this starts in the mind. Your attitude towards life has everything to do with your spiritual growth.

BITTER OR BETTER

Years ago I visited an encounter group in a psychiatric hospital. What I saw there shocked me. The people were filled with bitterness, hatred, anger and unforgiveness. Their attitudes were actually the reason why they were in that mental hospital. They were not physically ill—they were emotionally ill.

What was so interesting is that these people were very rational about everything—right up to the point where each started talking about one particular person or situation. Then they would just go bananas.

One woman I spoke with had just been brought into the facility the day before. She told me she was a Christian. I asked why she was there, and she began to tell me her story. "My husband left me for another woman. He married her and they're off traipsing through Europe. I'm left with no money—not enough to feed my children or myself. I can't ... I can't...." She couldn't finish her sentence. Bitterness just swept over her face.

Without question, her husband had done a rotten thing. But what struck me was that while he was off enjoying himself, she was sitting in a mental hospital—all because she had allowed him to devastate her life. I say "allowed" because she alone permitted the attitude of bitterness to creep in and take over her emotional state. She let this happen.

I have known the Lord long enough to know with certainty that if this woman had turned over her bitter feelings to the Lord and trusted Him, He would have brought forth miracles for her. He would have delivered her out of the bondage of bitterness and provided for her children.

The people I met in that mental hospital had been dealt a rough load. But a lot of them didn't know God. They didn't know the strength and comfort God can give—that He's ready to give. We need to fill ourselves with God's promises in His Word so when those hard times come, we're prepared. We want our attitude in trials to reflect the peace we have through Jesus.

PASA CHARA

James gives us very clear direction about the purpose of trials, and about the attitude with which we're to face them.

> My brethren, count it all joy when you fall into various trials, knowing that the testing of your faith produces patience. But let patience have its perfect work, that you may be perfect and complete, lacking nothing (James 1:2-4).

I want you to read this portion of Scripture over and over. Let it permeate your mind. In particular, repeat those four words: "count it all joy."

The *Amplified Bible* translates James' words this way:

> Consider it wholly joyful, my brethren, whenever you are enveloped in or encounter trials of any sort, or fall into various temptations. Be assured and understand that the trial and proving of your faith bring out endurance and steadfastness and patience. But let endurance and steadfastness and patience have full play and do a thorough work so that you may be people perfectly and fully developed with no defects, lacking in nothing.

Lastly, I think it's just precious the way *The Living Bible* expresses it.

> Dear brothers, is your life full of difficulties and temptations? Then be happy. For when the way is rough your patience has a chance to grow. So let it grow, and don't try to squirm out of your problems, for when your patience is finally in full bloom, then you will be ready for anything—strong in character, full and complete.

I have to confess that when I'm going through some difficulty, I don't much like it when people tell me to be happy. "Be of good cheer!" they'll say. I don't like to be told that, but I know it's true. It's a matter of attitude.

In one of his commentaries, William Barclay says we're to "reckon it all joy." [11] The idea there is to look at it like bookkeeping. These days, we have all sorts of computer programs which will keep your books for you, but before these came along we had to have actual books with a column for the debits and a column for the credits. Barclay is saying we're to put trials on the credit side. We're to reckon or count it as joy.

Another commentator said James 1:2 actually begins with the Greek words for "all joy." The Greek word for "all" is *pasa*, and it means the totality of things, wholly and completely. Consider everything you go through in your pilgrimage on this earth all joy—all the good and all the bad. "Joy" in the Greek is *chara*. I got to thinking how fun it would be if we started our letters or e-mails with "*Pasa Chara.*" Or maybe that would be a great way to sign off. They'll think you're really brilliant if you do that.

LOOK PAST THE TRIAL

Now, when I suggest you look at every single circumstance in your life and you count it all joy, you might think, *She's crazy. She doesn't know what I'm going through or she wouldn't suggest that.* I may not know all the particulars of what you're going through, but I do know very well what it is to walk through dark, dark trials. Over the years we've had our share of pits, despair, darkness and disaster, but God allowed us to go through each thing so we would gain compassion to share with others.

James isn't telling us that the trial itself is all joy. Disaster is never joyful. But when we look past the trial at all the good things that will result, we can endure the hardship with joy. When you see the words "count it," say to yourself, "Think forward, consider or regard it." If you can look beyond the immediate trial, you will get a glimpse of the wonderful things God will produce through it.

Remember Jesus,

> The author and finisher of our faith, who for the joy that was set before Him endured the cross, despising the shame, and has sat down at the right hand of the throne of God (Hebrews 12:2).

It wasn't the pain of the crucifixion that would give Jesus joy. It was what the crucifixion would do. Through His suffering it would bring life to us. And He looked forward to the life we would receive and the victory over Satan. That was the joy set before Him.

It's like the athlete who exercises strenuously and constantly adds more weight to make the exercising more difficult so he can look forward to great big, rippling muscles and all that extra endurance and strength. That's what trials do in our lives. They strengthen and mature us.

AN ATTITUDE OF GRATITUDE

So when trials appear unexpectedly, how should a Christian woman meet them? Well, first you need to be aware that one of two things will happen. Either the external pressure you've just encountered will have a good effect on you, causing you to grow in Jesus, or it will have a bad effect on you, causing you to go backwards. External pressure causes an internal attitude. What attitude are the pressures in your life forming in you right now?

I read a little story in Edith Schaeffer's book, *Affliction*, [12] in which she gave an illustration of a woman who was run over by a car. She said a person lying on the road after such an accident doesn't say, "Thank You, Lord, that this car ran over me."

But you do need to develop an attitude of thankfulness in your heart, because as Philippians 4:6 tells us, we are to make all our requests be made known to God with an attitude of thanksgiving. We look for the things in that situation we can thank God for. Remember the times in the past when God has met you and provided what you needed. Tell yourself it will happen this time too. Thank God ahead of time for the good you know He will bring.

This is one of the secrets that will keep you from ever having a mental breakdown—always be thankful, and keep remembering the things God has done so you can be thankful.

I strongly encourage you to begin a book of remembrances in which you can write down your prayer requests and then record the answers as God gives them. Then, when you find yourself in a situation so difficult that you can't see your way through, you can read your book of remembrances and say, "God worked a miracle there and He worked a miracle here. God is going to work a miracle in this too. He won't leave me in this place. He'll help me grow."

Do you remember what God did for the children of Israel when their thirst drove them to complain against Moses? "Did you bring us out of Egypt to die of thirst?" they asked him. Moses didn't know what to do. He only knew to bring the problem to the Lord. And God acted. He brought forth water from a rock at a place known thereafter as Meribah (Exodus 17:1-7).

Are you thirsty today? Do you feel you're out wandering in the desert with no hope of relief in sight? Remember that God is there. Look back on the Meribahs of your past and remember all the times He's brought forth water to satisfy your thirst.

Psalm 30:5 tells us, "Weeping may endure for a night, but joy comes in the morning." What a beautiful promise! No matter how things look at this moment, you can let joy lead the way and go before you. Your night of weeping will give way to a joyful morning. Knowing that, you can count it all joy now.

THE PURPOSE OF TRIALS

Now, when you look at James 1:2 in the *King James*, it says, "My brethren, count it all joy when ye fall into divers temptations." The Greek word translated "divers" there means "a variety of colors." I think that opens up a new way to understand this verse.

Have you ever thought about your temptations in terms of color? Think about the things we associate with different colors. We sometimes say, "She was as white as a sheet." White denotes an attitude of fear. What color goes with depression? Well, when we're down we usually say we're feeling blue. How about anger? That would be the color red. Sometimes things come up that tempt us to indulge those very emotions—fear, depression, or anger. The temptation is there, but we don't have to fall into it.

The word "temptation" comes from the Greek word *peirasmos*, which means "testing." It has the meaning of a trial that is directed towards an end. The diverse temptations that come along our path always have a purpose. The purpose is not to seduce you into sin or destroy you, but to purify, prove and strengthen you. It's like a young bird leaving the nest and testing its wings.

Remember God promised Abraham that his seed would be as the sand of the sea. But he grew impatient. Lacking trust in God's promise, he took Hagar and conceived a son of the flesh. But somehow, by the time Abraham's son of the promise, Isaac, was born, Abraham's faith had been so strengthened by the trials he had endured that he was able to offer up his promised son on the altar. He had so much confidence in God, he was able to obey what God had asked him to do. He knew that if he had to slay his son, God would bring him back to life.

Don't forget the purpose of temptations. They are not allowed into our lives to make us fall, but rather to make us soar like the eagle. They are not to defeat us, but that we might defeat them. They are not sent to make us weaker, but to make us stronger. God uses them to remove the impurities, which weaken us and make us unusable. Just as gold is purified by being put through the fire, so we are purified through the testings we go through. Impurity of any sort weakens gold and keeps it from reflecting as it ought. It's been said that the refiner will keep burning the impurities out of the gold until it's so pure, he can see his own reflection in it.

Do you wonder why you're in the fire of testing today? Maybe there's some impurity there, some dross God is trying to bring out. The Refiner allows us to go through testings over and over and over until He sees His reflection in us. Isn't that what we want too—to reflect the face of our Father to a dying world?

TRIALS STRENGTHEN FAITH

Another beautiful promise concerning this is found in 1 Peter 1:6-7.

> In this you greatly rejoice, though now for a little while, if need be, you have been grieved by various trials, that the genuineness of your faith, being much more precious than gold that perishes, though it is tested by fire, may be found to praise, honor, and glory at the revelation of Jesus Christ.

Your faith, tried by the fires of trials, will result in praise, honor and glory on that day Jesus reveals Himself.

Not all of our trials originated with us. Job's testing did not originate with him—it originated with Satan, who went before God and said, "That man over there won't keep serving You. He won't be faithful. You can't trust him. If You touch his body and allow him to have sickness, he'll curse You" (Job 1:6-22). To prove God had a man who was faithful, who really loved Him and could be trusted, God allowed Job to go through these fires. So sometimes the trials are not of our own doing.

But sometimes they are. Sometimes you refuse to be obedient to God in the flesh, and yet your spirit cries out to Him and says, "Oh God, I want to be purified. I really want to walk with You." Though you can't seem to get victory over the flesh, your spirit is willing to go through the refining fire, so God allows a testing to come.

A close friend of mine lost her husband quite suddenly. I had been at the hospital with her day after day as he was in critical condition. As I was driving home one night I said, "Lord, why are You taking him? He loves You. He serves You. His family needs him. His wife needs him. Lord, what are You doing?"

God spoke to my mind and said, "I'm proving her faith." He was, and that was not the end of it. That dear friend of mine has gone through trial after trial after trial. Her faith has been tried over and over and over, but she is coming out as pure gold. She has never once railed against God. Oh, she's cried a lot, and she's carried on a little bit, and she's had some very sad, very bad days. But she has never once turned her back on God or lost assurance that He was at work in her life. If we're to be women who reflect God, we will each go through testing.

Maybe that's why Peter tells us not to be surprised when those trials come.

> Beloved, do not think it strange concerning the fiery trial which is to try you, as though some strange thing happened to you; but rejoice to the extent that you partake of Christ's sufferings, that when His glory is revealed, you may also be glad with exceeding joy (1 Peter 4:12-13).

You're not the only person going through fiery trials. Many members in the body are going through fiery trials today—through persecutions, through heartaches, through sickness, through loneliness and all kinds of external hardships. Every bit of it is working a refinement in their lives.

TRIALS PRODUCE PATIENCE

Looking at James 1:3, we read, "Knowing that the testing of your faith produces patience." In the margin of your Bible, next to that word "knowing," write "Recognize this." When you begin to go through a hard time, you need to stop and recognize that God is working something out in your life.

A trial is simply an instrument to accomplish God's purpose for you. At the conclusion of every trial, you will have either moved forward, spiritually speaking, or you will have moved backward. If you moved backward—if you resist the changes God wants to work in you through the trial—then you will likely have to go through a similar trial down the road. God will keep working in you until you learn what He wants you to learn.

The person who is able to "count it all joy" is the person who will develop patience in her trial. The word "patience" means "to stay, to abide, to be steadfast, or to stand fast." The more a tree is tossed about by fierce winds, the deeper its roots go. We need deep roots. We need to be rooted and grounded in Him, and these trials cause us to dig into the soil with our roots and stand taller and firmer.

If you never had any trials, you'd be a weak, obnoxious Christian. The most difficult people in the body of Christ are usually those who haven't yet had a trial. Because they haven't been tested, they tend to be like a child who demands to be the center of attention all the time. But those who have learned the art of abiding under pressure are able to go through life without breaking under the strain.

If you were to see a blacksmith at work, you would notice he holds a piece of iron over the fire until it becomes very pliable. Then he's able to bend and shape it any way he wants. The metal he starts out with is unyielding. It could never be used to make a horseshoe. But in the heat of the fire, it becomes usable. Can you see how God is using these trials to make you pliable? He's causing that stiff, unyielding person that you once were to become the softened, sweet, loving person He intended you to be.

The Living Bible translates James 1:3 this way: "For when the way is rough, your patience has a chance to grow." That's just simple and true.

I remember when our grandson, William, who was just little at the time, spent the day with us. Of course, being with Grandpa was like a visit to Disneyland—just fun, fun, fun. Anything William wanted, William got. So he said, "Grandpa, I want to stay at your house a long time." Grandpa said, "Well, William, you have a nice home." William said right back, "Oh Grandpa, it's rough there."

It really wasn't rough at William's house. He just had to go through a few small fiery trials at home, as we all do. When he was with Grandpa he didn't have to. I think being with Grandpa was a little taste of what heaven's going to be like. When all our fiery trials are over, we're going to look back and say, "Wow, it was rough there." But by then, we will have come forth like gold.

TRIALS PRODUCE MATURITY

"But let patience have its perfect work, that you may be mature and complete, lacking nothing" (James 1:4). William Barclay describes the patience being produced as "unswerving constancy." [13] I like that: unswerving constancy. *The Living Bible* says, "So let it (patience) grow and don't try to squirm out of your problems."

We like to squirm out of our problems, don't we? We like to run. But running can get you swallowed by whales. Jonah would tell you that it's never worth it to try to run in the opposite direction (Jonah 1). Squirming doesn't pay.

The purpose of all trials is to move us toward maturity—"that you may be perfect and complete." God is growing you into a mature, fully-developed adult, and He uses tests to fit you for the tasks you were sent to do in this world. A lack of hardships makes for a spiritually-immature Christian. Knowing this should help us face our trials with the right attitude. I truly believe the attitude we take toward our trials will either make us mature and usable for God's work or it will make us unfit and unusable.

We testify of God by our attitude in trials. What does the world think of God when they hear one of His people whining, "Why did God allow this to happen to me?" On the other hand, imagine what the world thinks of God when they watch you going through a fiery trial and they hear you say, "This is painful. I'm hurting. But I know I can count it all joy, because God has a purpose and a plan. When I come out of this, I'm going to be stronger. I'm not going to break under the strain of this life."

I remember once just before Chuck and I were to leave for a trip to New Guinea, our daughter, Cheryl, asked us to go on a hike with her. She had found a really beautiful spot and wanted to show it to us. So off we went, and let me tell you, it was an unbelievable hike—clear up to the very top of this high hill. It was a long walk, and the whole time we were on the trail I was thinking how great it was, because with all that perspiration rolling down my face, I just knew I was going to lose some weight.

But better than that, I knew I was strengthening my muscles for our trip to New Guinea. Even though I wasn't sure exactly what awaited me there, I wanted to be physically fit to endure it. The walk itself was hard—which is always the case when the weakness of the flesh is being burned off—but I knew joy awaited me at the end of it. And that makes all the difference between an attitude of complaining and an attitude of worship.

The last part of verse 4 really sums up God's desire for you: "that you may be perfect and complete, lacking nothing" (James 1:4). Lacking nothing. Do you realize that's what God wants for you? He doesn't want you deficient in anything at all—not morally weak, not spiritually weak, not without integrity, not without purpose in life. He wants you to know the blessing and the peace that comes from being steadfast and unmovable, always abounding in the work He has prepared for you.

Finally, there's another precious promise in James 1:12, which says,

> Blessed is the man who endures temptation, for when he has been approved, he will receive the crown of life which the Lord has promised to those who love Him.

Isn't that beautiful? As the King's daughter, you will receive the crown of life. Believe it today. Believe it and act on it.

Father, we know it is only through the strengthening of the Holy Spirit that we can face trials and hardships with faith. We want our attitude in those times of testing to speak of Your love and Your power. We want our behavior to reflect our faith in You. We ask for Your strengthening. We ask that You work in us an unswerving constancy.

In Jesus' name. Amen.

7

SHE IS LOVING

ON THAT FINAL NIGHT before He was betrayed, sometime after Judas rushed from the upper room, Jesus took the opportunity to give a few last instructions to the disciples. As they sat together around the table, He said,

> A new commandment I give to you, that you love one another; as I have loved you, that you also love one another (John 13:34).

He then told them it would be this one quality by which the world would judge their discipleship.

> By this all will know that you are My disciples, if you have love for one another (John 13:35).

Jesus had spoken to them often about love.

> You shall love the LORD your God with all your heart, with all your soul, and with all your mind. This is the first and great commandment. And the second is like it: You shall love your neighbor as yourself (Matthew 22:37-39).

AGAPE LOVE

The fact is, if we love God as we should, we will be able to love others as we should. We'll be able to walk morally and socially as representatives of God. The love Jesus described is *agape* love, a Greek term meaning a love that lays down its will, its rights—and even its own life—for the sake of another. Probably the best description you can find of this kind of love is found in 1 Corinthians 13:4-7—a passage I strongly encourage you to memorize.

> Love suffers long and is kind; love does not envy; love does not parade itself, is not puffed up; does not behave rudely, does not seek its own, is not provoked, thinks no evil; does not rejoice in iniquity, but rejoices in the truth; bears all things, believes all things, hopes all things, endures all things.

But *agape* love is not limited to the New Testament. This was not a new concept. Moses taught about that kind of love in Deuteronomy 6 when he gave the Ten Commandments to the children of Israel. The first four of those commandments concern love for God, and the last six tell us how we are to love our neighbor. Summed up together, they fulfill the Law. As Romans 13:10 tells us, "Love does no harm to a neighbor; therefore love is the fulfillment of the law."

There's no more beautiful picture of *agape* love than what we find in John 3:16, "For God so loved the world that He gave His only begotten Son, that whoever believes in Him should not perish but have everlasting life."

Out of His great love for us, God willingly gave His most prized possession as payment for our sins. This is the deepest love ever shown to mankind. As we read in that passage from John 3, it's a love we're commanded to show towards one another.

Agape love differs from the kind of love mentioned in Titus 2. When Paul wrote to Titus that the older women are to teach the young women "to love their husbands, to love their children" (Titus 2:4), the word he used for love is *phileo*. We are to *phileo* our husbands and our children.

On the topic of loving your husband, you can walk into any Christian bookstore and find dozens of books on specific things you can do to improve your marriage. You'll find tips on how to cook a romantic meal, how to dress your table with candlesticks, and the best ways to greet your husband at the front door. There's no lack of suggestions for those sorts of things. But what I want to tell you in this chapter deals with the very root of that word *phileo*. It goes beyond setting a pretty table or cooking a fantastic meal. It goes to the heart of what it means to be loving.

Now, you might be reading that last sentence and thinking, *I already know how to be loving.* That may be true. But this is a topic for all women— young women, older women, women who are hearing this for the first time, and women who have walked with the Lord for a long, long time. It never hurts to be reminded of these truths. Think of this as being a refresher course. Who doesn't need one of those once in a while?

PHILEO LOVE

First, let's look at the word itself. *Phileo* is a verb. It's an action word meaning "friendly love." *Phileo* carries the idea of being friendly to another; taking delight in or longing for that person. It represents tender affection. This is the kind of love God wants you to have for your husband, your children and for other people in your life.

Keeping that definition in mind—a love that takes pleasure or delight in another—ask yourself if that is a true picture of you. If you're married, would your husband say that you take delight in him? Would he say you are friendly toward him? What about your children? It is quite easy, most of the time, to feel friendly toward your friends. But what about those in your family? Think honestly about your answer to these questions. This may be an issue you need to bring to the Lord.

Titus clearly tells us we are to "*phileo*" our husbands and our children. But that's not the only place where we'll find that word in the New Testament. The writer of Hebrews used *phileo* when he wrote, "Let brotherly love continue" (13:1). Paul used *phileo* in Romans 12:10 when he said,

> Be kindly affectionate to one another with brotherly love, in honor giving preference to one another.

In closing his letter to Titus, Paul wrote,

> All who are with me greet you. Greet those who love us (*phileo*) in the faith (Titus 3:15).

The apostle Peter used *phileo* when he wrote,

> Since you have purified your souls in obeying the truth through the Spirit in sincere love of the brethren, love one another fervently with a pure heart (1 Peter 1:22).

I want to focus on that last verse for a moment. In this example of *phileo* love, Peter is very obviously addressing believers. But *phileo* love is not exclusively a Christian love. Unbelievers can and do have this kind of affectionate fondness for one another.

But if you want to demonstrate the kind of *phileo* love described here—a love that reflects God's own emotional fondness and affection for you—then you need to "purify your soul in obeying the truth through the

Spirit." An unbeliever cannot have a pure heart. Only a heart that is indwelt with the Holy Spirit can be purified to love with this kind of fervency.

The New Strong's Dictionary makes a distinction between *agape* and *phileo*:

> PHILEO = (fil-eh'-o); to be a friend to (fond of [an individual or an object]), i.e. have affection for denoting personal attachment, as a matter of sentiment or feeling; while (*agape*) is wider, embracing especially the judgment and the deliberate assent of the will as a matter of principle, duty and propriety: the two thus stand related; the former (*phileo*) being chiefly of the heart and the latter (*agape*) of the head. [14]

GENUINE LOVE

God wants you to love others with both your head and your heart. If you learn to look at others with your head—seeing them as children of God who are deeply loved by Him, regardless of their faults and flaws—it will only enhance the emotions of your heart. You will find even more motivation for loving your husband, your children, your friends, your mother-in-law, or your son- or daughter-in-law, and your neighbors. It won't be hard because your head and your heart will be working together to demonstrate a love that reflects God's love for them.

It's so important for us to understand these truths about genuine love. So very often in marriage, when one or both spouses have a wrong idea about what it means to be loving, the marriage begins to operate on a bartering system. Everything becomes reciprocal. "If you do this for me, then I'll do that for you." And the reverse is true. "If you don't do this for me, I won't do that for you." We withhold and we punish and we play games. "He didn't kiss me good-bye? Well, then ... tonight ... zero!"

That's not genuine love. Real love—the kind that Jesus demonstrated—is not reciprocal. It's completely unselfish. Maybe you know this, but it's a struggle for you. Maybe you're very aware of what God is asking you to do, and you want to do it to please Him, but you don't know how. I want to give you three steps to becoming a more loving person—a person who reflects God to everyone He brings into your life.

STEP 1: BE IN A RIGHT RELATIONSHIP WITH GOD

Pure, genuine love comes from a heart that is born again. Apart from the indwelling of the Holy Spirit, you will not be able to demonstrate the kind of love that Jesus did—a love that puts others first and is willing to sacrifice self for the sake of someone else.

A lot of times women will hear a lecture or read something in a book and they'll think, *Hmm. That sounds interesting. I'm going to try that out on my husband.* But your husbands can tell the difference between actions that come from a deep love and actions that come from just a "let's see if this works" kind of attitude. By the way, this is true of friends, children and other family members too.

Motivation is everything. If you try out a new recipe for your husband because you want to please him, and he ignores it, you think, *He must not like that one, so I won't make that one again.* You're not personally offended, because it wasn't about you—it was about pleasing him. That's serving out of a deep love.

But if that's not your motivation, and you set some new dish in front of your husband and he ignores it or fails to praise you for it, anger rises up and you feel like grabbing that plate and tossing the contents in the garbage disposal.

If the interior life is right, the exterior life will be right. But if the interior is phony, it will show on the outside. No matter what you try to do to minister to others, it will fall flat. People can tell the difference.

STEP 2: CHECK YOUR ATTITUDE

If you want to love as Christ did, then you must not hang on to un-Christlike attitudes and feelings toward others. In other words, Christ's *agape* love as set forth in 1 Corinthians 13:4-6 must be at work in your life. I've repeated this Scripture to help you commit it to memory:

> Love suffers long and is kind
> Love does not envy
> Love does not parade itself, is not puffed up
> Love does not behave rudely
> Love does not seek its own
> Love is not provoked
> Love thinks no evil
> Love does not rejoice in iniquity
> Love rejoices in the truth.

There's no room in a loving heart for unforgiveness, resentment, anger, or bitterness. No matter how deeply someone else may have wronged you, these attitudes will only block the flow of love.

Paul warns us about the devastation that bitterness can cause.

> See to it that no one misses the grace of God and that no bitter root grows up to cause trouble and defile many (Hebrews 12:15 *NIV*).

One of the dangers with bitterness is how quickly it can spread to others. For instance, if you have children and they see your bitterness towards someone else, they pick it up from you. Or your husband will see that you're bitter toward someone, and he'll become bitter toward that person too.

Bitterness is dangerous and it is grievous to God. That's why it's wise to check our hearts frequently to see if we've allowed a root of bitterness to begin to grow.

As Psalm 139:23-24 says in *The Living Bible*,

> Search me, O God, and know my heart ... point out anything You find in me that makes You sad.

Anything that grieves God must go. He is ready to help you. Jesus provides release from every attitude and every feeling that is not from Him. Your part is to confess your feelings to Him honestly—remember, God already knows the truth.

If you want assurance of His omniscience, read the rest of Psalm 139. He knows everything about you. So confess your feelings truthfully and ask Him to forgive and heal you of the wounds that will be left after the removal of that bitterness and resentment. You can't just put a band-aid on those kinds of wounds. You need a healing balm. Thank the Lord Psalm 147:3 tells us, "He heals the brokenhearted and binds up their wounds." Don't you love that?

FORGIVE AND PRAY FOR OTHERS

Now, after you've confessed your bitterness and you've gone to God for healing, pray for the person who has hurt you. Ouch! That's hard. But it's also necessary. Pray and ask God to meet his or her deepest emotional needs. Even if you don't know what those needs might be, you can be sure every person has deep emotional needs which can only be met by God. Maybe the person who hurt you is a single mom raising children alone. Maybe it's a widow. They all have their own particular needs, and the God who created them is the only One who can meet them. He knows just how to provide circumstances that fulfill it.

The more you pray for that person, the easier it will become. You do it by faith and see it as a completed work. Refuse to think angry, ugly thoughts about the person. Satan loves to bring up those hurtful things again and again. "Remember how that person hurt you?" he'll whisper. Don't listen.

One of the most beautiful aspects of love as described in 1 Corinthians 13 is that love doesn't keep account of wrongs done. Love is not a book-keeper, jotting down all the bad things people have done against you.

God gave me a tool for these situations that has helped me immeasurably. When I'm trying to forgive someone for a hurt they've done to me, I picture that person before the throne with the light of God flowing through them. His light dispels darkness. It warms people, cleanses them, and changes them.

We have to remember that those people who have hurt us are God's responsibility. I've had to say that to the Lord now and then. "Lord, they're Your responsibility." That's what Moses reminded God when the children of Israel started complaining and carrying on against Moses in the wilderness (Exodus 16:2). "God, they're Your children. They're Your responsibility." And they are.

It also helps to remember that none of us are perfect yet. We are all in process. If you look at someone who has hurt you and you realize that one day, that person will stand before God in heaven and he or she will finally be who they were created to be, it changes your perspective. It really does. It makes it so much easier to forgive them and love them.

Think of it—one day we all will be perfectly matured in Jesus. And we'll stay that way forever! We need to look at each other not as what we are—with all our funny failures, our craziness, disappointments, all our hurts and heartaches, and the way we wound one another—but as God sees us right now, through Christ Jesus. We are perfected in Him.

FORGIVENESS IS NOT OPTIONAL

Now, sometimes the harm done to us is so great or so vile that we have a very hard time giving up our feelings of resentment or bitterness. If that's where you find yourself, gaze upon Jesus. Take a long look at your

Savior, who was despised, rejected, reviled and even crucified—yet He never stopped loving us.

I think that's what caused Stephen to react the way he did when he was being stoned to death. He had gazed at Jesus and learned from Him, and as he was dying at the hands of his enemies, he prayed forgiveness for those people. Stephen's last words were, "Lord, I pray that You lay not this sin to their charge" (Acts 7:55-60).

Forgiveness is not optional. We need to forgive just because the Lord tells us to do so. But if you want a selfish reason to forgive (one that will eventually work unselfishness in you), do it for your own health.

In the last decade or so, doctors and scientists have been conducting "research forgiveness" to determine the physical effects of unforgiveness. [15] Any number of physical reactions happen when we hold on to unforgiveness: muscle fatigue, headaches, constriction of blood vessels, reduction of oxygen and nutrients to the cells, interruption of sleep, jaw problems from clenched teeth ... and the list goes on.

So for your own good, choose forgiveness. Choose it today and choose it every time someone crosses your will. It would be nice if it was a one-time decision and it lasted forever and suddenly you loved everyone and life was just beautiful and marvelous all the time. But it's not like that. Forgiveness is a continual work. It's a daily work.

Every time someone crosses you and those angry feelings spring up, you have to go to the Lord right then and there and ask Him to work His love for that person in your heart. We live in an imperfect world with imperfect people and a wicked adversary who enjoys trying to destroy relationships, so you're going to get lots of chances to practice forgiveness.

WALK IN FORGIVENESS AND LOVE

Going back for a moment, marriage seems to be one relationship Satan works overtime to try to destroy. That's because the Devil wants to rob you of your wholeness and make you an emotional misfit.

Maybe you're at that place right now. Maybe things have gotten so bad in your marriage that you're like the woman who was described as an "emotional porcupine." She had so many bristles her poor husband couldn't get near her. Often this is the case when a woman is married to an unbeliever. He might be a workaholic, or an alcoholic, or he might be unfaithful to her. Maybe he's cruel.

If you're in this situation and you've been a believer for any time at all, you probably know 1 Peter 3:1 backwards and forwards.

> Wives, likewise, be submissive to your own husbands, that even if some do not obey the word, they, without a word, may be won by the conduct of their wives.

The problem is, you can know the verse and just grit your teeth and determine to live out that verse, but unless you have pure love flowing through you to your husband, you'll never be able to obey that verse. You can't put the cart before the horse. The love has to come first, and then the actions will follow.

First, go the way of the cross, and then you'll have a quiet-enough, gentle-enough, loving-enough conduct that you'll begin to truly minister in a way that will bless your husband and please the Lord. Apart from that, there is no power to fulfill this verse. I've seen over and over again a wife who is so naturally filled with bitterness toward her husband that she begins to crave revenge. She wants to get even, no matter what it takes.

Sometimes a woman will think the best way to get revenge on an unfaithful husband is to be unfaithful herself. But that's a fruitless, destructive choice. All that does is make it much harder to repair your marriage. If you want God to flow through you to reach your husband, then you must put aside your bitterness and be filled instead with His Holy Spirit. Leave the changing of your husband to God. You do your part—walk in forgiveness and love—and leave the responsibility of your husband to God.

And for those of you who are unmarried, this message is for you too. If a family member, friend or co-worker has upset you—walk in forgiveness and love towards that person. Pray for them and allow God to be the One to change them. In the meantime, you just be a reflection of Jesus.

Now, if you've allowed yourself to get all bristly like that porcupine woman, you might not even have a desire to forgive at this point. So you need to ask God to begin the work. You just say, "God, I know my attitude is wrong. I ask You today to give me the desire to forgive." God is faithful. You can rely on His faithfulness. He'll begin that work in you, and one day, all of a sudden, there will be a little glimmer of light. You'll start thinking, *Maybe I should work on forgiveness a little bit.* Then a little more will come, and a little bit more, and before you know it, you'll find yourself walking in love.

STEP 3: STUDY THE ONES YOU LOVE

In order to reveal your love outwardly, through your attitude and your actions, you must first know how that other person needs to hear "I love you." This takes some detective work. As someone once said, "What good does it do for you to say 'I love you' if it's not the way I need to hear it?" Now, what you may not do with this information is to reverse it and use it against your husband. I'm not dealing with husbands in this book. This is for you.

One of the reasons why marriage books don't work for every single marriage is because there's not a one-size-fits-all love language. Every person needs to hear it differently.

I had a friend whose husband thought she was at her most desirable when she wore a great big Mother Hubbard flannel nightie. He just couldn't leave her alone when she wore that big old nightgown. Now, most husbands would not say they find Mother Hubbard flannel nighties irresistible. That's not the usual advice. So books on marriage are not going to steer you toward the flannel sleepwear. They're going to tell you to wear something slinky or lacy instead.

I remember one book suggesting that you put on a baby doll nightie and long white boots. Can you imagine? But if my friend were to have picked up that book and followed its suggestion, her husband would have been disappointed. He hears "I love you" with flannel. So there you go.

Unless you hear love expressed in a language you understand emotionally, it will have little value to you. When you buy a gift for someone, you think about what that person is like, what they could use, what they would enjoy. If their favorite color is blue and their most-hated color is gold, you don't buy something painted gold, do you? No. You look for something blue.

So too, it's important in marriage for you to speak love in a language that your spouse understands and appreciates. Maybe he likes to hear "I love you" with words, just like that. Maybe he likes for you to surprise him with a gift, or with an act of service. Maybe he hears "I love you" when you touch him, or when you spend time with him. Whatever it is, that's what you do.

We begin determining who loves us right from infancy, and it continues on through childhood. However our parents loved us, and others close to us, will determine our love language. When people speak that particular language to us, we believe they love us.

For the rest of our lives, this has become our yardstick. It's our measuring tool. And we apply it regularly to our most important relationships to see if anything has changed since last week, or yesterday, or whenever we last checked. We have to know: Does he love me as much today as he did in the beginning? Or with our friends: Are we closer now than we were last year?

Every woman needs those kinds of assurances. It's the way God made us. But it's interesting that most of us spend more time measuring how much we are loved rather than measuring how much we are loving. Wouldn't it be better if we took our yardsticks and applied them to ourselves?

LOVE OBSERVATIONS

In his book, *The Secret of Staying in Love*, John Powell wrote that we need to watch each other with the look of love. [16] That means constantly reading the needs of the other.

You look at your husband and ask yourself, "Who does he need me to be this morning? Who does he need me to be tonight? Is he discouraged today? Does he need my strength in any area?" Sometimes, when our husbands are down or discouraged, the most loving thing we can do is to strengthen them with our encouragement. Or if they're lonely, what they need is for us to put our hands softly in theirs. Have you ever just walked up and taken your husband's hand? You can say so much through that one simple gesture.

I remember back when I used to play the piano at church, and Sunday after Sunday, Chuck and I would be so busy with our different ministry tasks that it felt like we were going in completely different directions. Sometimes we hadn't even had a chance to say hello. But every Sunday morning as he walked by the piano, Chuck would always put his hand on my shoulder and give it a squeeze. It said more than an hour's worth of conversation. In just that one gesture he communicated the caring and love that I needed. It was so precious to me.

Other times, when our husbands have experienced some success or accomplishment, what they need most is for us to celebrate with them. Oddly, some wives have allowed a wall to build in this area. They simply cannot or will not rejoice with their husbands. Usually with a little digging you find that resentment has built those walls. As we've already discussed, there's no room for resentment in the heart of a believer. Get rid of the resentment and begin loving your husband in the language he needs to hear.

If you're unsure of your husband's love language and he's not giving you any clues, just ask the Lord. Our God is both omniscient and creative. He knows what your husband's love language is and He knows how to plant creative thoughts within you and open your eyes to the things that matter most to your loved one.

DO IT TO PLEASE GOD

The first ten years of our marriage, I didn't bother to read Chuck much. He was so controlled, so secure and confident … he was my Rock of Gibraltar! I leaned on him and felt rather dependent upon him. I had absolutely no idea what was going on inside him, nor was I worried about it. Chuck will tell you he's never been depressed a day in his life—and I believe it—though he has gotten discouraged now and again. But he was brought up to never show negative emotions, so he didn't. If he was upset or angry, he kept it to himself.

I would encourage him in my own way if I suspected he was a little discouraged. I'd say something like, "I love you, you darling thing, you," without ever wondering if that was what he needed to hear or if it would minister to him. In the back of my mind I was pretty sure he didn't even need me to say it. But God began to tell me differently. As I prayed, He began to show me creative ways to tell Chuck that I loved him.

I've always loved perfume. Even when we were living on fifteen dollars a week, I figured out ways to get perfume. But Chuck would never say a word. Even now, after sixty years of marriage, the only way he's ever remarked on my perfume is if I first asked him, "Do you like this?" Usually his answer is, "Like what?" He just has never really noticed perfume. But one summer day, back before we knew we shouldn't do such a thing, I was out tanning and I rubbed olive oil on my skin. When he came home and kissed me hello, he said, "Ahhh! What is that?" He loved the olive oil! I never could have figured that out for myself. But God knew what Chuck liked! And He found a way to let me know too.

If you are married, learn what pleases your husband. That's what you do with a friend, right? And we want to have that friendship, *phileo* love for our husbands. It's been said in surveys that men will admit the number one thing they want in marriage is companionship—not intelligence, not a sense of humor, not great beauty. Companionship. Are you being a companion to him? Are you being a loving friend?

We want to learn these things to bless our husbands. But more than that, we want to learn these things (and do them) because it pleases God. There's no greater motivation than that. It encompasses so much more than just the marriage relationship.

The same principles that apply to marriage apply to relationships with our children, our parents, our neighbors, and our friends. If you can get this one concept down, you'll have all the motivation you could ever need for loving others with that *phileo* love. Do it for the Lord. Do it to please His heart.

After all, pleasing God is the reason for your existence, and for mine. As we're told in Revelation 4:11,

> You are worthy, O Lord, to receive glory and honor and power; for You created all things, and by Your will they exist and were created.

You were born to please God. Will you do that? When you do, your love for others will reflect Jesus.

Father, I ask that You fill us with so much love for You that we live every day with Your pleasure in mind. Teach us to forgive. Teach us to be loving.

In Jesus' name we ask. Amen.

8

SHE IS A FRIEND

FRIENDSHIP IS SUCH A VITAL, beautiful part of the human existence. Where would we be without those precious relationships? God created friendships to exist between two humans, but He also created friendships to exist between Himself and us. It's true.

In Exodus 33:11 we read, "The LORD spoke to Moses face to face, as a man speaks to his friend." Second Chronicles 20:7 describes God as being Abraham's "friend forever." And in John 15:15 Jesus said, "No longer do I call you servants, for a servant does not know what his master is doing; but I have called you friends."

God is our supreme Friend. And when we love others with that same kind of empathy, concern and care, we are simply reflecting the Lord's heart.

In the last chapter, we talked about the need for *phileo* or friendship love. In this chapter, I want to describe for you the specific characteristics of a woman who knows how to be a friend.

Before I give you that description, though, I'd like to ask you to assess yourself. When you read each of these traits, ask yourself if you see this within you. Maybe it was there at one time, but life has buried that trait in you. That happens sometimes.

In a marriage, after those first romantic feelings begin to wane, disillusionment can set in. We forget to be a friend to our husband or to have delight in him. This can even happen with our children. They're so adorable when we bring them home from the hospital. But when that same baby wakes us up night after night and we walk around feeling perpetually tired, the pleasure we felt at first can quickly diminish.

Children need a lot of care and they are capable of making some pretty big messes. They have a way of denting furniture and spilling food all over the floor. All that washing and cleaning and picking up can rob us of our pleasure in those little ones. Irritation replaces joy. We can easily become so distracted by tracked-in mud that we lose the wonder and enjoyment of these lives whom God has entrusted into our care.

We want to take stock of all our relationships and ask God to help us to be the best friend we can be. I have written an inventory list describing seven traits of a woman who knows how to be a friend. This is not a complete list. I'm sure we could add more traits to these seven. But these are just a few of the traits we want to develop so that our loved ones—and a watching world—will see the heart of God reflected in us.

118

1. SHE IS LOYAL

Chuck once gave me a perfect definition for a loyal friend. He said, "It's somebody who is for you." Isn't that what we all need—to know that someone is in our corner?

Let me ask you this: Whose corner are you in? Who are you loyal to in your life? I hope you have some very close friendships—that no matter what happens, your friends know you will always stand by their side.

Let's talk about your family for a moment. Do you let your husband and your children know you are there for them? Do they understand that you will be behind them no matter what they do?

I hope you can say yes to these questions—because too many wives these days act as if they are against their husbands and their children. They talk behind their loved ones' backs, they gossip about their faults and complain about their behavior. Basically, they tear down their loved ones in front of other people.

Every husband has the right to expect loyalty from his wife. Proverbs 31:11 speaks of the virtuous woman and tells us, "The heart of her husband safely trusts her."

A husband who has this kind of wife has a friend. She's careful with the details of their marriage. She doesn't tell others when he throws his socks on the floor and neglects to put the cap back on the toothpaste. She doesn't complain about his "dumb ideas" when he decides he wants to paint the house purple. That is a dumb idea, come to think of it, but she doesn't run around telling other people about it. No, she asks God for the grace to go along with his plans.

Now, I want to be careful to explain here that I am not talking about a marriage where there is really a broken relationship, and the husband has become abusive and cruel. If you're in a marriage like that, you need help. You have every right to go to someone for counseling. But if that's not your situation, be careful whether you're with your husband or apart from him, that you're not picking, picking, picking at everything he wants to do.

But this is for every woman who has a close relationship with a friend, a sister, a daughter, a roommate, or a co-worker. This applies to you. Be a loyal friend.

2. SHE IS A LOVING LISTENER

A good friend is someone you're not afraid to entrust with your dreams, your plans and your hopes. You gladly share those things with your friend because you know he or she won't ridicule or lecture you. You're not afraid to confess your mistakes, because that person has proven to be a sympathetic listener.

The people closest to you in your life ought to have that kind of freedom with you. They should be able to come to you with their ideas, their big plans, their broken hearts, or their remorse over a wrong choice. They should be able to tell you anything without risking an unwelcome lecture.

Think about a little child who bursts into the back door to announce, "Mom, I walked through a muddy pool today because it was just so much fun!" What happens if this mother greets that announcement with comments like, "Oh! You should not have done that! Why would you do that? Don't you know you can get a bad cold?" What happens is the child tucks that lecture away in the back of his mind, and he determines he'll never share his muddy pool adventures with his mother again. Not ever.

We can just instinctively blurt out all the wrong things. It's so easy to be negative! But if we keep our goal uppermost in our minds—that we want to reflect the heart of God by being a friend to our loved ones—we can catch ourselves and turn our comments around. Instead of being a mother who shuts down her child or a wife who shuts down her husband, you can be a friend. Learn to be a listener.

Take to heart the words of James, who said, "Be swift to hear, slow to speak" (James 1:19). Proverbs tells us that's wisdom. "He who restrains his lips is wise" (Proverbs 10:19). And she who restrains her lips is wise.

I'm not telling you that it's wrong to correct your child, or offer sound but contrary advice to your husband or to a friend. Sometimes those conversations are necessary. If your child, for instance, tells you she did something wrong, there's a definite place for offering wise advice. But you have to be wise about when you offer this wise advice.

Later, after you've had time to think and pray and squelch the lecture, you can sit down and say, "You know, I've been thinking about what you shared with me, and I was wondering what the result would have been if…." That's the way to offer your suggestion. Who couldn't take that kind of gentle advice?

I have actually known some husbands who refuse to share anything with their wives. In fact, each husband has reached a point where he barely even communicates with his wife anymore. I've also known children who will not share anything of importance with their mother because they know everything leads to a lecture. I don't want that to be you. If you need to shape up in this area, then do it. Stop lecturing, stop looking aghast at everything they bring to you, and start listening.

3. SHE IS CARING
A friend is someone who cares about you and what happens to you—and it shows. If you're hurt, they're hurt. If you're blessed, they're blessed. The woman who wants to reflect God by being a friend will live out the truth of 1 Corinthians 12:26:

And if one member suffers, all the members suffer with it; or if one member is honored, all the members rejoice with it.

I remember a time when our house was just a beehive of activity. Our daughter Janette and her husband, Greg, had sold one home and they were waiting to get into the next, so they were living in a motor home in the front of our house with their daughter, Caitlyn. At the very same time, Jeff and Cheryl were still living at home, and between both of them, they had lots of friends coming and going. Sometimes our bedroom felt like our own little private hideaway.

I remember one morning when Chuck said to me, "You know, I think we should always have extended family here. I love it! Everybody coming in and out." It was so sweet.

We never knew who might show up. Cheryl brought home a friend one day and was introducing us, and she gave me a first name only. I kind of laughed and said, "What's her last name?" Cheryl stopped for a second and then said, "Mom, I don't know." It was like that at the house—lots of activity and it was all very precious and fun.

During this time, little things happened and big things happened. At one point, one member of our family had something happen that seemed a bit tragic to them, and we were all there to show support. Everyone was so caring and sympathetic. Don't we all need that? It seems so glaringly absent in our society.

It's so important that you learn to reflect God by being a friend to your family and loved ones. They need it. They need to know you care. They need to know that when they come home from a long, exhausting, depressing day, they've come home to a safe, loving, supportive place.

Are you careful to show this kind of love to your family? When they come home at the end of a day, do you ask how the day went? Do you try to read their body language to see if they're okay? These are things a friend would notice. A friend will look for little gestures they can give to show their support.

Do you write little notes (if your husband is the kind who would like that) and put them in his lunch bag or on the steering wheel of his car? It takes so little time to write a note, but it can make all the difference in how someone starts their day.

Do you ever give your husband or your children a Scripture? When you have your prayer time in the morning and you're praying for them, does the Lord ever give you a special verse just to share with them? That evening or the next morning you can say, "Oh honey, when I was praying for you this morning, the Lord gave me this sweet Scripture for you." Maybe it's Joshua 1:9:

> Be strong and of good courage; do not be afraid, nor be dismayed, for the LORD your God is with you wherever you go.

Wouldn't that be a great way to start the day? Or you could just write, "I love you," or words that will reflect God's love to your husband or your children. It means so much

4. SHE IS FUN TO BE WITH

Proverbs 17:22 tells us, "A merry heart does good, like medicine." Isn't it delightful to be around someone with a merry heart? Laughter has a curative effect on the body. Something about laughter just helps you to relax.

Don't you find it refreshing to spend time with a friend who knows how to have fun and how to be fun? Well, consider this: as much as you enjoy this in others, your friends and family members need it too. And they need it from you.

Maybe you're thinking right now, *I'm not like that at all*. Maybe your conscience is telling you that you're prone to be irritable, cranky and morose. It's not too late to change. Meditate on that verse from Proverbs and ask God to work it into your life.

When you think of this trait, the first relationship you think of might be one which you have with your adult friends. Of course, this trait is absolutely important in those relationships. But did you know that it's important in your closest relationships too? If you're a wife, your husband wants and needs to have fun with you. If you're a mother, your children need to have fun with you too.

When your husband thinks about spending time with you, he should look at it as a revitalizing time. He should look forward to your companionship, knowing that your presence will "do good, like medicine."

Do you think your husband feels that way? Or is he on guard because he knows you're going to use that time to list his inadequacies and bring up all the things he hasn't done? "You're neglecting me! You watched TV for four hours last night and hardly even spoke to me!" Of course, if that's true, it is negligence. But it's wrong to try to manipulate your husband through your complaining. God is not pleased with manipulation. He is pleased when you remember that your husband is His responsibility, and you back away in faith and entrust the changing of your husband to God.

Instead of heaping burdens on your husband—or guilt, conviction or regret—try to lighten his load when you're with him. Ask the Lord to show you how you can bring some fun into your husband's life.

The same goes for your children. Do you know how to create fun for your little ones? It's so lovely for children to have a mother like that. Hardly anyone feels comfortable around someone who is constantly nagging you to straighten up or pick up your clothes or get your elbows off the table. How many moms spend dinnertime correcting or lecturing their kids? Don't do it. There is a time and place to have those kinds of corrective conversations. Dinnertime is not that time. Make dinnertime fun.

Often when my children were little they used to tell us how much they loved dinnertime because we did so many fun things. We used to have Bible quizzes while we ate dinner. Or we would just go around the table and ask, "What happened today that was the most fun to you?" Some days they didn't have anything happen that was fun. Those were the days when they needed an extra touch of love, caring and sweetness extended to them.

Part of being a fun mother is keeping the wonder alive for your children. Take those little ones for a walk, and remember that you're not zooming to get somewhere just so you can turn around and zoom home. Be willing to stop and look at a caterpillar, a butterfly or a flower. If you live near the ocean, take them down to the beach and stand at the edge of the water together. Talk to them about God's majesty and His power. Pick up a scoop of sand and tell them that God created every particle—that His thoughts toward them are more than the grains of sand of all the beaches of all the oceans in the world (Psalm 139:17-18). Let them know how great God is.

Wise is the woman who learns how to bring fun into her own life, and into the lives of those she loves.

5. SHE IS QUICK TO PRAISE AND APPRECIATE

I think if we were to keep a list for one week of all the times we criticized and all the times we expressed approval or admiration, we'd be shocked. In a study done years ago, two psychologists lived in a home with a family for a while, keeping track of that very thing. At the end of their evaluation, they found the ratio of criticism to approval was six to one. Can you believe that? For every admiring comment, the parents made six critical comments.

We are so prone to finding fault. For whatever reason, many of us have a very difficult time expressing admiration or appreciation. Think about the people you are the closest to. When was the last time you told your friend you thought she was wonderful? How about your husband or children? Did you start out the morning telling them how special they are? "There's nobody in the world I love as much as you." Or "Did you know you're my special gift from God?"

It's true, you know. It doesn't matter how difficult they might be at times. They are your special gift from God, and they have a right to know that. They have a *need* to know that. Has it ever occurred to you that they might be God's special gift to you, if only to train and teach you?

One of our pastors, Don McClure, used to say that his mother became an intercessor because of all the trouble he put her through. I have found that to be true. My children have taught me more about myself than anything or anyone else ever did. I learned that God still had a lot of work to do in me!

The truth is, we take a great deal for granted. If you're married and your husband heads out to his job every morning, do you ever stop to tell him how grateful you are? "Honey, thank you for going out and working and bringing home a paycheck and being faithful in your job." If he's not working regularly (or at all), maybe you could help him along by becoming an encourager. Maybe you haven't shown a lot of appreciation in the past.

Your precious children need this same kind of encouragement. My dad was probably the best example in the whole world of a person who showed appreciation. Chuck had the best mother in the world and I had the best father, so we entered marriage with high expectations for each other!

My mother could be pretty hard on me. I know it came from a place of concern, but sometimes she was far too firm. If I was practicing the piano and she thought it sounded rotten, she'd tell me so. But my dad would say, "That's beautiful!" If he really thought I needed to work on something, he'd say, "Catheryn, this is very good, but I know you can do even better." He put so much love in his comments that I constantly wanted to do better to please him.

My handwriting, for instance, was atrocious, but he kept working with me until I finally learned to write more legibly. No matter what I brought home from school, he took time to look at it, appreciate it and comment on it. His encouragement was such a special, special blessing to me.

Show encouragement and appreciation to your children. When your kindergarteners come home with crumpled up papers in their hands, take a moment to admire them. Do it verbally! I used to tack them up on the wall so I could see them all through the day. Even now, every so often I get those papers out and look at that sweet little lettering and too much paste all over everything … so very precious. Oh, keep them! Tuck them away someplace safe. When you get to be my age and your children are grown up, you'll look at those and be so blessed.

6. SHE IS FLEXIBLE

The Living Bible phrases 1 Peter 3:1 in an interesting way:

> Wives, fit in with your husbands' plans.

You're never going to hear this advice from the world. In fact, this notion of adapting yourself to the plans of your husband runs counter to everything the world would have you believe. But there's something very beautiful about a woman who is willing to be a friend to her husband in this way.

You will also make yourself a friend to your children by learning to adjust yourself to their individual temperaments. Not every child responds to the same thing, the same way. Children have different learning styles, for instance. If your child is one who loves order and routine and long-range planning (and some of them do), don't frustrate them by insisting that they adjust to your preferences.

Maybe you prefer to think about tomorrow when tomorrow gets here. You can't be bothered with calendars, organizers and schedules. But in order to be a friend to your child, allow them their own calendar, organizer and schedule. You adjust to them. Or if you have a child who needs to touch-and-do in order to learn, don't insist that they learn everything by sitting in a chair and reading a book. Let them get their hands messy. You can create learning opportunities for them that appeal to their own learning style.

I would say children give us the most opportunities to learn flexibility. How many mothers know what it's like to have a baby wake up from his nap long before you expected he or she would do so? Probably every mama. But here's where love flows through flexibility. You squelch those thoughts of, *Oh, I had so much to do during his nap!* Instead of allowing yourself to feel frustrated, you adapt. You run to the crib and you cuddle that baby and tell him, "I'm so glad my baby's awake! I missed you!"

I once heard an interview with a teacher who won an award for being the best teacher in her district. One of the questions they asked her was, "How are you so patient with all those children?" She answered, "When I'm prone to get impatient, I look at their little feet. I just glance down and I think, *Oh those little feet have such a long journey.*"

They do, you know. Be patient with them, you mamas. Be patient and be flexible.

Think for a moment about how friendly you'd feel toward one of your adult friends if everything always had to be done their way—if they never considered your needs or your likes and dislikes, and they refused to compromise or allow you to choose once in a while. You probably wouldn't have that friend for long, would you? It's the same with your husband and your children. If you want to be a friend to them, you need to learn to be flexible so you can adapt to their wants and needs.

7. SHE IS ACCEPTING

A woman who knows how to be a friend doesn't force her loved ones to be prisoners of her own expectations. What I mean by this is that she doesn't say, "I will love you *if* ... *If* you do such and such ... *If* you will jump through all my hoops ... I will love you *if* you behave ... but *if* you don't behave, I will not love you." It's the difference between conditional love and unconditional love. Think about this: If Jesus loved us conditionally, we probably wouldn't be loved at all, would we?

I was at a summer camp once and I saw this little boy standing in the dining hall line. While he stood there he started throwing dirt. Out of nowhere, a woman walked up to him and said, "If you keep that up, Jesus won't love you!" That just hurt my heart so much! I couldn't help but jump into that conversation. I said, "Jesus *will* love you. He'd just rather that you not throw dirt, I think." I couldn't leave that horrible concept in this child's heart. But you don't want those ideas in your husband or in your children either.

Love the people whom God has entrusted to you, and accept them as precious works in progress. Psalm 139:14 tells us all that we are "fearfully and wonderfully made." Each woman who picks up this book is a unique, special, wonderful being. And each husband and child represented by each of you is also unique and special. They might behave in ways that are painful. They might not yet be where they should be. But remember this: although we can't see the end from the beginning, God can.

And "He who has begun a good work in [your husband, your child, your loved ones] will [not might—*will*] complete it until the day of Jesus Christ" (Philippians 1:6).

God is in the process of bringing that one to Himself. When you give conditional love, you block the flow of God's love to that man, or that child, or to that friend.

Get rid of the "if only's." Accept your loved ones just the way they are, with all their little naughtiness and all their little difficult places and all those things that make you crazy. Tell them you love them right now, with no strings attached.

THE REASONS WHY

Why is this so important? Well, it matters for a couple of reasons. Number one, it pleases the heart of God when you are a loving, friendly reflection of Him. But it also brings blessing to your own life. You're building a house, you know. It doesn't happen all at once or overnight.

Sometimes it can be hard to see any progress at all. But every time you lay aside your own agenda or your own preferences for the sake of your loved ones, every time you bite back a critical remark and replace it with an encouragement, every time you slow yourself down enough to say "I love you" to the ones God has entrusted to you, you're building your house. Someday, when it's all finished, it's going to be beautiful.

Proverbs tells us, "The wise woman builds her house, but the foolish pulls it down with her hands" (Proverbs 14:1).

Which woman do you want to be?

And number two, this matters because the stakes are so high. Children can grow up scarred. Marriages can fall apart.

I once talked to a man who was preparing to divorce his wife. We tried to encourage him to forestall the proceedings and work on his marriage, but he went through with it anyway. The problem? His wife tore him down continually—privately and in front of other people, she constantly labeled him a failure. "He's always been a failure and he always will be a failure," she'd say. With one side of her mouth she'd tell him, "I love you," but with the other she'd complain, "You'll never succeed at anything you do." Oh, if that woman had understood some of these concepts! How different the outcome might have been.

The stakes are tremendously high for your children too. Did you know that when you speak to your children, you are holding a mirror in front of them? Whatever you say to them determines who they believe they are. If you tell them you love them, they believe they are lovable. If your words are harsh or unloving, they believe they are unworthy of love.

A child subconsciously thinks, *If my mother doesn't love me, nobody's going to love me.* When Cheryl was a little girl, she was sitting on my lap one day when she looked up at me and said, "Mama! I can see me in your eyes!"

It's never too late to become a friend. Ask God to help you and start today. This is the day of new beginnings for you and your loved ones. Take pleasure in each one. In so doing, you will take those first steps toward building a lasting legacy.

Proverbs 31 reads,

> Her children rise up and call her blessed; her husband also, and he praises her ... Charm is deceitful and beauty is passing, but a woman who fears the LORD, she shall be praised (Proverbs 31:28, 30).

One day your husband and your children will rise up and call you blessed. Even better than that, you'll please the heart of your Father, when you reflect His friendship to the world.

Father, You are our closest Friend. You are the Friend who sticks closer than a brother. May we learn to love others with that same friendship love, that we would display Your beauty to everyone You have entrusted to us. Anoint us with Your Holy Spirit, that we would have Your eyes to see each one with grace and unconditional love.

In Your precious name we ask. Amen.

CHAPTER

9

SHE IS OBEDIENT

WHEN SOMEONE SAYS THE WORD "obedience" to you, what thoughts come first to your mind? Do you have a negative reaction to that word, seeing it as something insufferable or unpleasant? Or do you understand the power and beauty of obedience?

Throughout the Bible, we're admonished to obey God. Over and over, the writers of Scripture, under the inspiration of the Holy Spirit, urge us to obey all that is written in God's laws. God inspired them to give us those exhortations for several reasons. One reason is that obedience brings blessing to your life.

Observe and obey all these words which I command you, that it may go well with you and your children after you forever, when you do what is good and right in the sight of the LORD your God (Deuteronomy 12:28).

Proverbs tells us very clearly that blessings await the ones who listen and obey.

Listen to Me, my children, for blessed are those who keep My ways. Hear instruction and be wise, and do not disdain it. Blessed is the man who listens to Me, watching daily at My gates, waiting at the posts of My doors (Proverbs 8:32-34).

And the psalmist tells us,

Great peace have those who love Your law, and nothing causes them to stumble (Psalm 119:165).

OBEDIENCE IS A WITNESS

But obedience doesn't just bring us personal blessing. It also makes us an effective witness in the world.

Therefore, my beloved, as you have always obeyed, not as in my presence only, but now much more in my absence, work out your own salvation with fear and trembling; for it is God who works in you both to will and to do for His good pleasure. Do all things without complaining and disputing, that you may become blameless and harmless, children of God without fault in the midst of a crooked and perverse generation, among whom you shine as lights in the world, holding fast the word of life (Philippians 2:12-16).

When we obey God, we shine brightly in this dark world and we reflect Him. Our lives look different, because we're not living to please ourselves but to please the Lord. And this is so important if we want to reach the lost. If our lives do not look different to the world, they have no reason to reach out for God.

One of the areas where obedience most distinguishes us from the world is in the area of marriage. I want to talk about that in this chapter, but first I want to make it clear that, regardless of your station in life, you are called to be obedient.

The single woman is to be an effective witness in the world just as the married woman. One will display her obedience through her devotion to God and her happy submission to His Word; the other will display her obedience through those two things as well, but she will also witness to the world through her willingness to submit to her husband.

The fact is, I've noticed whenever I've studied the topic of marriage with my ladies in the Joyful Life Bible Study, [17] that the lesson applies equally for the single women as it does for those who are married. It seems that these principles apply to your daily walk regardless of your marital status.

So this chapter is definitely for you if you're married. But if you're single, widowed or divorced, there's a lot in here for you too. As Isaiah 54:5 says, "For your Maker is your husband, the LORD of hosts is His name." For those of you who do not have an earthly husband, take these principles and ask God to work them into your life so you can love and serve Him even more.

Obedience to God's Word is one way we can acknowledge His lordship in our lives. When we obey, we are saying that He knows better than we do about how we should live. God knows better than we do how to live a single life that honors Him, and He knows better than we do how to live a married life that honors Him. So really, all we need to do is obey the things He has written in His Word.

PROTECTION FROM DECEPTION
When it comes to marriage, you can be certain that God knows much more about men than you do, and He knows what they need in their

marriage. Many of you might not agree, but if God's Word says it, you need to accept it. If you find something in Scripture that you feel rebellious against, you need to realize that you are rebelling against God Himself. Remember that and realize you cannot please God if there is rebellion in your heart.

One of the passages that causes the most rebellion in the hearts of women is Ephesians 5:22-24:

> Wives, submit to your own husbands, as to the Lord. For the husband is head of the wife, as also Christ is head of the church; and He is the Savior of the body. Therefore, just as the church is subject to Christ, so let the wives be to their own husbands in everything.

The question this always brings up is, "Why?" Women want to know why man was made head over the woman.

Paul gives us the answer to that question in 1 Timothy 2:12-14:

> And I do not permit a woman to teach or to have authority over a man, but to be in silence. For Adam was formed first, then Eve. And Adam was not deceived, but the woman being deceived, fell into transgression.

Now, I don't believe that women are more easily deceived in everything. But I do believe they are more easily deceived by Satan. That's the only explanation I can find for why some women marry the men they marry or get themselves involved in the other messes that they do—choices that ruin their lives and their reputations. They're deceived, just as Eve was when she took the fruit Satan offered her. The result of her transgression is set forth in Genesis 3:16:

> To the woman He said: "I will greatly multiply your sorrow and your conception; in pain you shall bring forth children; your desire shall be for your husband, and he shall rule over you."

One of the consequences of Eve's sin was that her husband would rule over her. For this reason, I want to warn you single girls not to marry someone whose wisdom and judgment you don't trust and whom you are not able to obey.

PROTECTION FROM HARM

This puts a heavy responsibility on the man, because part of his job is to keep his wife from being deceived. I do not view this as a punishment to the woman but as a protection for her. During the trip that Chuck and I took to New Guinea, we noticed when married couples walked down the road, the man would walk five to ten feet in front of his wife, carrying nothing but a spear or a bow and arrow. The wife, though, would be loaded down with all kinds of things. Each and every one of the kids would be clustered around her as she would be bent over with big bundles upon her back. It looked just awful.

I said to Chuck, "Boy, who wants to be a New Guinean wife?" But then it was explained to us. Do you know why the husband walks ahead? He does it to protect his wife and children. If a snake or a wild animal or some other enemy were to suddenly appear, and the husband's hands were full of other things, he couldn't protect his family.

I see an application here for the married woman. Are you putting burdens on your husband he doesn't need to carry? Are his arms so full of things you're supposed to be carrying that he can't really protect you? Sometimes we wives expect too much from our men. They want to protect us, but we won't let them.

I used to be such a patsy when people came to the door selling things. I couldn't say no, and I didn't use any good sense or wisdom about it. So one day Chuck finally said, "Kay, don't buy anything from the door." He said, "I don't care if it's just a shoestring. Don't buy anything from the door." He also said, "You may not have any Stanley Home Parties." Do you know what they were? They were home parties where all your friends would gather and you'd buy Stanley products. They were so much fun. But Chuck said, "You may not have any Stanley parties in our house." He said, "It might be right for other people, but as a pastor, I feel it's wrong for us. You are not to invite anybody here ever to sell them anything at any time."

Now, whether I liked the rules or not, they turned out to be a wonderful protection for me. You would be amazed at the reaction I got when somebody came to the door to sell me something and they heard, "My husband says I can't buy anything from the door."

"Your *husband* said?"

I would say, "Yes, and he's about this tall and this big!" I've learned that obedience pays. It's been a real help. It's so much easier than hearing door salesmen's big, long spiels and having to fight my impulse to want to help them out by spending money.

Chuck has protected me in other ways as well. Back when our four kids were little, it became very difficult for me to do everything that needed doing at church and to still get everything done at home. Chuck made it easier for me when he said, "Kay, you are to be a wife and mother first." That meant the church came third.

Church for him had a different place on his priority list, but for me, it came after my responsibilities as the wife and mother. It was an amazing protection for me. Before he said that, I felt like I had to be at every church function that came along. I didn't feel that I could say no. But he freed me up to relax and enjoy my time with our children.

Again, you see where obedience is a protection for you. I've often wondered what would have happened if Adam had protected Eve from Satan's temptation. And I'm not too sure that Genesis 3:16 wasn't also a punishment to Adam for not doing so. It's as if God said, "Listen, you've got to rule over her and she's not going to like it. She won't want to submit. It's going to be a lot of *fun* for you." And now all that *fun* has been passed down through the generations to us. Ooh!

SARAH'S EXAMPLE

I realize that not all husbands assume the leadership role they should. Sometimes women will say, "I'm more spiritual than my husband, and I have a lot more sense. What do I do about that?" If you want to see a wonderful example of a woman who continued to obey even when her husband didn't show the best leadership, look at Sarah.

Abraham was not the best husband—he really wasn't. He moved his wife away from everything that was familiar to her, and to a country they knew nothing about. She was sixty-five at the time. Who among us would like to start over at sixty-five? Then he let his selfish nephew choose the best land for his own. Doubting God's promises of a son through Sarah, he took her handmaid, Hagar, and had a child by her. Even though that was Sarah's idea, a man of strong, godly leadership would have said, "Sarah, sit down, be quiet. You're going to bear the child—forget Hagar." But Abraham didn't. Twice, for his own protection, he lied about Sarah being his wife and pretended that she was just his sister.

Life with Abraham wasn't easy. In fact, it must have been extremely difficult. Sarah could have resisted everything Abraham wanted to do. We tend to think that women in her day had no options, but she could have returned to her family and refused to journey with Abraham.

When he lied about her being his wife and made her vulnerable to the pharaoh and to King Abimelech, she could have had a fling with one or both of them. Apparently, Sarah was quite good-looking. It must have been flattering to her to have both a king and a pharaoh after her—and when she was an old lady, no less! She could have had a rather nice life in the palace, don't you suppose? Why travel all over the country with Abraham when she could live in a palace? And then—she has a baby at ninety-one! (Genesis 17:17). Who wants to do that?

Read 1 Peter 3:5-6.

> For in this manner, in former times, the holy women who trusted in God also adorned themselves, being submissive to their own husbands, as Sarah obeyed Abraham, calling him lord, whose daughters you are if you do good and are not afraid with any terror.

Sarah obeyed Abraham and called him lord. She was not afraid and trusted her husband.

OBEDIENCE HONORS GOD'S WORD

God can deal with your husband and He can change him, but you need to get out of the way. Chuck has spoken about this many times from the pulpit. He talks about what happens when a woman stands in the place of judge and accuser with her husband, constantly pointing out to him all the things he should and shouldn't be doing.

Do you know what happens? That man may have been feeling some guilt or some conviction of the Holy Spirit about his behavior, but his wife's behavior does away with all that. Because she has already punished him with her nagging, his guilt is alleviated and he no longer feels a responsibility to God.

It is so important for you to remember this—if you alleviate your husband of his guilt, he will never come to the place where he feels responsible to God for his behavior. Your husband is not your responsibility. He is God's responsibility. Move out of the way and put him in a position where God can deal directly with him.

Now, the Lord might use you. He might give you words of wisdom or words of kindness. But you can be sure He will never use you to accuse your husband and rant and rail against him. The best thing to do is to get out of the way and let God work.

When we obey our husbands and submit to their leadership, God's Word is honored. When we do not, however, we bring dishonor to God's Word.

Titus 2:5 tells us to be "obedient to our husbands, that the word of God may not be blasphemed."

In the *New International Version* it says, "So that no one will malign the Word of God."

And the *New American Standard Bible* translates it, "That the Word of God will not be dishonored."

The *Amplified Bible* gives us a detailed description: "That the Word of God may not be exposed to reproach (blasphemed or discredited)." We do not want our behavior to bring blame to God or misrepresent Him to the world.

GOD'S PURPOSE FOR MARRIAGE

Have you ever asked yourself about the purpose of marriage—about the purpose of *your* marriage? Many women have a wrong perspective about this. They believe, mistakenly, that marriage exists to make them happy. They picture marriage as their own Cinderella story. But Cinderella's story is not true. The only way to correct that perspective is to stand back a bit and look at marriage from God's perspective.

God has redeemed the world at a great cost to Himself, but the world does not know it. He desires to manifest that redemption to a lost and hungry world, and marriage plays a part in this. A marriage that lines up with biblical principles beautifully displays God's redemption. So whether or not your marriage is happy is beside the point.

Your marriage is an opportunity for you to reflect God's work in the world. If He can better bring His purposes to pass by breaking my heart or your heart, then we must thank Him for this. Maybe God is going to bring a witness to the world through you that nothing else could have brought. This is joy, but it cannot be understood unless you are in love with Jesus Christ.

Paul said,

> But thanks be to God, who in Christ always leads us in triumph [as trophies of Christ's victory] and through us spreads and makes evident the fragrance of the knowledge of God everywhere (2 Corinthians 2:14, *Amplified Bible*).

God designed marriage as the symbol of Christ's love for the church. It's a symbol to the world of Christ's redemption. This is so evident when you read the fifth chapter of Ephesians. Look at it again with these concluding verses.

> Wives, submit to your own husbands, as to the Lord. For the husband is head of the wife, as also Christ is head of the church; and He is the Savior of the body. Therefore, just as the church is subject to Christ, so let the wives be to their own husbands in everything.

> Husbands, love your wives, just as Christ also loved the church and gave Himself for her, that He might sanctify and cleanse her with the washing of water by the word, that He might present her to Himself a glorious church, not having spot or wrinkle or any such thing, but that she should be holy and without blemish.

> So husbands ought to love their own wives as their own bodies; he who loves his wife loves himself. For no one ever hated his own flesh, but nourishes and cherishes it, just as the Lord does the church.

For we are members of His body, of His flesh and of His bones. "For this reason a man shall leave his father and mother and be joined to his wife, and the two shall become one flesh."

This is a great mystery, but I speak concerning Christ and the church. Nevertheless let each one of you in particular so love his own wife as himself, and let the wife see that she respects her husband (Ephesians 5:22-33).

What a beautiful picture. Your marriage can be an opportunity to reflect God's love to the world.

When Paul wrote his letter to Titus, admonishing him that the older women were to train the younger women to love their husbands and children and to care for their homes, he did so because the Christian women at Crete and Corinth were flaunting their liberty in Christ by appearing in the streets with their heads uncovered. In that time and in that culture, this was a symbol of the prostitute.

In effect, these women were saying, "Now that we have liberty in Christ, we no longer have to be stuck in our homes, seeing only our husbands and our children and a few of our women friends. We can go out in the street! We can do whatever we want and we don't have to wear a veil anymore."

But the non-Christian world that saw this behavior was absolutely horrified. I think most of the world we know today does not admire a woman who neglects her husband and children. Maybe a radical few do. But the majority of the non-Christian world believes a Christian woman will be a faithful wife and a loving mother.

So if you aren't, then you are causing the Word of God to be blasphemed, and your marriage is not being used as the symbol it should be in this godless generation.

REPRESENTING GOD

God is always concerned about how you represent Him. The question to ask yourself is: How am I representing God? Do I readily obey all of God's commands, even the ones that make me uncomfortable? Am I willing to humble myself and take a lesser position? Do I give the world an opportunity to criticize the church or to admire it?

One of the greatest handicaps the church has is the witness of unsatisfactory lives of professing Christians. And one of the greatest arguments for Christianity is the evidence of obedience in genuine Christian lives. The world has nothing to compare to the beauty, joy and fellowship of a truly Christian home.

Nothing speaks more to this lost world than the Christian home. The home is on trial in the world right now. Marriages are on trial. The people outside are watching Christians to see if there is something in their marriages and their homes that is special, different and vital. They want to know if we have something they need. Is your life holding forth Jesus as the missing ingredient?

General Motors conducted a study that concluded the average person will strongly influence at least 162 people in his or her lifetime. The depth and breadth of your influence will be related to the quality of your marriage. If you represent your marriage as being crummy and your husband as being a cad, then the message you will give to those in your sphere of influence is that Jesus Christ isn't empowering you to have a peaceful home or a satisfying marriage. You're telling those 162 people that you have no contentment in your life. Do you think that will draw them toward Jesus or away from Him?

Maybe you've harbored rebellion toward God's Word or resentment toward your husband. If that's the case, I urge you to repent for the sake of the Lord Jesus Christ. Are you willing to turn from that rebellion and become the bondslave of Christ? Are you willing to obey the Scriptures by obeying your husband?

You may say, "Oh, Kay, you don't know my husband. You don't know what he's like. He's rotten to the core." That's not important. The purpose of Paul's admonition to be obedient or to be subject to your own husband was not to satisfy the capricious whims of a selfish man. It is for you to be a witness to the world by your behavior. It's to give you an opportunity to enhance your Christian testimony.

I am around an awful lot of marriages and when I see a woman who responds to her immature, neglectful husband with a sweet, loving spirit, my heart is touched. Isn't yours? When you see the beauty of God's grace enabling a woman to endure such a man and respond with kindness, it makes you want to be a better wife yourself. It makes you want to love Jesus and love your husband even more.

Now, I'm not suggesting you obey a man who is physically abusive to you or your children. I do not believe that you are required to stay in a marriage with a man who is destroying you physically. And you must protect your children even if your husband won't. But I'm not talking about that kind of situation.

I'm talking about enduring with grace when things are less than you might wish for—when your husband is not the leader he could or should be, or when he is distant or even cold. I'm talking about sticking with your marriage even when your heart is broken.

In those kinds of marriages, people will often say, "Don't stay in a marriage for the children's sake." As I said, in an abusive marriage where there is violence toward you or toward the children, that may be good advice. But in many marriages, it is that very thing—staying together for the sake of the children—that brings salvation to your husband or brokenness to you, so that you begin to cooperate with God and with each other.

A CROWN TO HER HUSBAND

Years ago when the book, *The Reproducers*, came out, it was full of stories on the beginning of Calvary Chapel and the wonderful testimonies about our time in the tent. [18] Now, when you look at a picture of a group of people, who do you look at first? You look at your own picture first, right? Well, it's no different when you discover you are going to be in a book.

The moment that book came out, I opened it really fast to find "Kay." But you know what "Kay" does in that book? She argues and sputters and debates with her husband. She is anything but submissive. That's not exactly what happened. I did cry a lot because I didn't want to move back to Costa Mesa from our church in Corona. I was wrong.

But still, when I saw the way that book portrayed me, I took it pretty hard. I cried and cried and cried. I wanted to be described as Chuck's lovely, gentle, soft-spoken wife, of course. But the Lord did not allow it. And I'm so grateful the book is now out of print. But God used that. One day when I was still thinking about that book, God said, "Kay, are you willing to be unknown?" I had to think about that. I had to let God use that situation and that question to break me.

Proverbs 31 is all about the virtuous woman. Verse after verse describes her wonderful traits, and then in verse 23 it says, "Her husband is known in the gates." The Proverbs 31 woman is this energetic, marvelous, glorious woman—but it's her husband who is known in the gates. The question before each wife is this: Are you willing to let your husband be known, even if that means you are unknown? Are you willing to be the kind of woman who is satisfied in being a crown to her husband? (Proverbs 12:4).

By being your husband's crown, you are signifying that he has authority. It's a beautiful symbol of honor. That's what you can be to him, but only if you're willing to obey the Scriptures by obeying him.

When you submit yourself to God's order and accept the structure He has established for your home, it is true that your husband will be the authority over you—but you will be very conspicuous as the crown on his head. Crowns are made of beautiful jewels with many lovely, sparkling facets, aren't they? That's what you can be to your husband. That's what your identity can be—the crown of glory upon his head.

Beloved, I urge you to stay in a place of obedience. In your marriage or in your singleness, let God bring forth His highest purposes for you in this great unfolding drama of the Lord Jesus Christ. May your life reflect the beauty of the Lord to all who are watching you—and may you influence them toward salvation.

Father, I ask You to do that deep work of repentance that will conform us to Your image. Show us how to live sacrificial lives, that through us the world will see the redemption of Jesus Christ. Teach us to obey, Father.

We ask it in Your holy name. Amen.

10

SHE KEEPS
HER HOME

WHEN MY MOTHER WAS twenty-four, her first husband died. She had a seven-year old daughter to care for at the time—my sister, Louise. So my mother, who was a very pretty woman, had to go out and work to support the two of them. She told me how she moved to Arizona and started a restaurant in a mining camp. At five o'clock in the morning when she'd be on her way to open the restaurant, she'd have to walk down the street with a gun at her side to protect herself.

Perhaps because of that experience, my mother did not want me to ever marry. Instead, she made sure I was trained for a career. She stressed this all through my growing up years: "Catheryn, have a career."

But then I got married. And I married a man who said, "No, Kay, I want you to stay at home."

Now, I want to state right up front that we live in an age and a culture where none of us has to marry. We have an option. No one forces us to marry—the choice is entirely ours. I want to say that very clearly, because as we go through this chapter, you might think I'm telling you marriage is the only way to go. I'm not. There are some very definite advantages to not getting married.

In particular, the Bible points out that,

> The unmarried woman cares about the things of the Lord, that she may be holy both in body and in spirit. But she who is married cares about the things of the world—how she may please her husband (1 Corinthians 7:34).

You may decide never to marry, but instead focus on walking closely with the Lord and learning to obey Him. That would be a beautiful way to spend your life. But if you do choose to marry, the Word tells us, as we just read, that you should desire to please your husband. And as we read in Titus 2:5, the young women who choose to marry are to be:

> discreet, chaste, homemakers, good, obedient to their own husbands, that the word of God may not be blasphemed.

OBEY YOUR HUSBAND

You are to be obedient to your husband. That's why you should never, ever marry someone you cannot obey. I don't think enough women take the time to realize the vows they are taking in their marriage ceremony, which is why too many girls choose poorly. They end up marrying men with poor judgment; men for whom they have so little respect that they can't bring themselves to obey them.

Somehow these girls get led away by how handsome he is or how much attention he pays to her. It's one thing or another and she talks herself into believing that he's "the one." She never takes two seconds to consider the fact that when she marries him, God is going to ask her to obey him. Remember, you have the option of whether or not to marry. But if you do, be prepared to obey your husband.

That's the position I found myself in when I married Chuck. I had my mother's admonition in my head—"Catheryn, have a career"—and my husband's conviction ringing in my ear—"Kay, I want you home." So I obeyed my husband. And I'll tell you over and over again, I have never been sorry. Not once. All our children are walking with the Lord. There is a fulfillment in that which is hard to describe.

It wasn't always easy and I didn't always sense that satisfaction. There were days when I felt trapped. There were days when I wanted to escape. There were days when the three oldest kids were in their teens and I took my Bible and just sat on the beach praying, "God, if You don't show me the way, I'm not going to make it." Those were crazy days. I had three teenagers at once and a little girl besides ... I was just not programmed for that and I really had to call upon God for wisdom.

We must keep in mind that our principal aim as Christians is to reflect God's heart, not our own. We want to bless Him in all we do and not give any occasion to the adversary to speak reproachfully against Him. So if the Lord says we are to obey our husbands, then we obey them (as long as they are not asking us to break God's laws). If God says we are to be homemakers, then we keep our home.

IDLENESS

What does it mean to keep your home? Well, in the simplest sense, it means that you attend to the physical needs of your home. Do the floors need to be swept or vacuumed? Do the clothes need to be washed? Do the dishes need to be done? Of course they do. If those things are not getting done, someone is not attending to that home. Diligence is lacking.

One of the main reasons why women do not attend to the basic needs of their home is they "eat the bread of idleness." This phrase is found in the description of the Proverbs 31 woman.

In verse 27 we read,

> She watches over the ways of her household, and does not eat the bread of idleness.

Now, the ladies in our Joyful Life Bible Study know well that I feel very, very strongly about one particular distraction. Actually, it's much more than a distraction. It's a destructive waste of time—soap operas. I am convinced that when a woman sits down and watches that ungodly filth, she is eating the bread of idleness.

I'd so much rather see you scrub a cupboard, clean out a drawer, work on a quilt, or even take the dog on a long walk. Anything but just sitting there filling your mind with that rot. So often when women are watching those shows, their little ones are playing in the same room listening to that same garbage. I'll say it again: Soap operas are nothing but a pollutant, and you know I'm right even if you feel rebellious against it.

So that's the first thing on my list. Chuck had another idea about this. He shared it with me when I was first teaching this topic to our ladies at Joyful Life, and I had asked him, "What things do you consider to be 'eating the bread of idleness'?" Almost without hesitation, Chuck answered, "Coffee klatches." That's not really a phrase we use these days, and Chuck doesn't even drink coffee, so I'm not sure what he knows about it. But I do think he's right.

As he said that, I remembered back in the early years of our marriage when women used to drop by for coffee. I was always pretty vigorous about wanting to get all my housework done and out of the way first thing in the morning. I wanted the beds made and the laundry washed before anything else happened. If the neighbors dropped by in the middle of my cleaning, I wasn't always as hospitable as I might have been. They'd come in for coffee and we'd sit at the table and talk, and often the talk was about things that would have been better left unsaid. It did seem like a waste of time.

You might have another thought about what is stealing your time. Do you allow yourself to waste hours on something that doesn't benefit your family or build you up in any way? These days, perhaps it's too much time on the Internet or on the phone. Whatever the bread of idleness represents in your life, cut it right out. Don't be a partaker of it. Don't give your time and energy to idle activities when you could—and should—be looking well to the ways of your household.

THE HOME ATMOSPHERE

Now, the physical needs of your home are probably apparent to you. Has it been a while since you tidied up? Is your house in order? When people walk in, does it seem clean to them? Those things are usually quite obvious. But something you might not automatically think about when you consider this topic of "keeping the home" is the emotional needs of your household. In other words, what kind of atmosphere are you setting for your home?

If we look again at Titus 2:5 in the *New King James*, we see that it admonishes the young women to "be discreet, chaste, homemakers, good…." That word for "good" is translated in other versions as "kind" or "kindly," and it means "to be tender, gentle, courteous, and considerate." Kindness is such a precious virtue in a woman—and such a blessing in the home.

My mom was always very courteous to my dad. When he came home in the evening, that was the special time of the day. There was one chair in our house that was "Dad's chair." If I happened to be sitting on it when he came home, I knew I was supposed to get up and let my dad have his chair. She taught me that.

When we ate, my dad was never, ever allowed to get up from the dining room table to get anything. My mom would get it or I would get it. That was just the way my mother felt the home should be, and she never complained about doing it. It was really beautiful watching the way she waited on him, and I learned a great deal of respect for my dad through her example.

Have you thought about the kinds of things you are modeling to your children? When they watch the interaction between you and their father, are they learning to be kind and courteous? Are they learning to be respectful? Or do you belittle him in front of the children or make him fend for himself?

Proverbs 18:21 tells us, "The tongue has the power of life and death" (*NIV*). I don't think we are mindful enough of that truth. The words we speak can either build up or tear down another person. They can model respect or teach disrespect to those little ones who are watching. Wise is the woman who chooses kind, tender words.

PRACTICE KINDNESS
Tenderness is such a beautiful quality in a woman. The alternative, you know, is to be a "tough" woman. I don't think most men like tough women. There should naturally be a quality of tenderness in us. We should be gracious and kind—not just to our husbands, but also to our children, our relatives, our friends, and the people in our church.

Proverbs says, "A kindhearted woman gains respect" (Proverbs 11:16).

Romans 12:10 admonishes us, "Be kindly affectionate to one another with brotherly love, in honor giving preference to one another."

Are you showing kindness in this way? Do you always rush out the door first or do you open the door and let your little ones go first? When you are with your friends, do you open the door for them? Do you choose the best seat in the car or in the restaurant or do you give that place to others? Do you prefer others above yourself in a conversation, or do you think you always have the best things to say?

Even if these things have not naturally occurred to you, you can begin right now to make a habit of preferring others over yourself.

Colossians 3:12 in *The Living Bible* tells us,

> Since you have been chosen by God who has given you this new kind of life, and because of His deep love and concern for you, you should practice tenderhearted mercy and kindness to others.

Practice kindness. Make yourself do it.

Proverbs 31:26 says this about the virtuous woman:

> She opens her mouth with wisdom, and on her tongue is the law of kindness.

I pray that more and more, this will be true for all of us who love Jesus. It's so easy to just blurt out a gruff comment, and then have to see that hurt expression on the other person's face. Oh, how it grieves the Spirit! At times like that, we really should bite our tongues. The last thing we want to be is a tough fishwife, screaming raucously at her husband, her children or her friends. That's a good image of what we do not want to be.

How would you describe the woman you want to be? Do you have an image of that woman? Do you see her treating everyone with gentleness and patience, always ready with a sweet, kind remark or a bit of encouragement? Let that be your goal. Ask the Holy Spirit to develop those qualities in you.

PATIENCE

Now, part of attending to the atmosphere in our homes is watching ourselves to make sure we're showing patience with our children. When my children were young, I used to go to the library and get books that described what children were supposed to be able to do at that age. And you know what? It really helped. It was amazing how much more patience I had with them when I kept their abilities in mind.

When our granddaughter, Caitlyn, was two, her family was staying with us for a time while their house was being built. I had somehow forgotten how exhausted you could be at the end of the day when you've spent it with a two-year-old. You're running after them here and there and their little moods are fluctuating all over the place—laughing one minute and crying the next—and just about the time you adjust to one emotion, another takes over. Let me tell you, I was being re-educated.

But then we spent some time with another two-year-old during this same period, and that child behaved the very same way. Then it came back to me. Chuck Jr. and Jeff were like that at two. That's just the way they are. It's good to remind ourselves of these things. It goes a long way toward making us gentle, patient mothers—or grandmothers.

STAYING HOME

A few major things have changed since I had young children at home. First, this generation is more apt to postpone having children, or decide completely against having children, than my generation. When I was a young wife, it was assumed you would begin a family. And I have to say that I am absolutely for Christian women bearing children.

I think we need all the Christians we can possibly get on this earth. And there's something so beautiful about seeing a baby born into a Christian home. So if you've been thinking about it, let me encourage you to have those babies.

The second major change in this generation is that more than ever, women feel pressured to have a career. Women had careers too when I was a young wife, but not to the extent they do today.

Because of all the improvements in gadgets and appliances, housework is not nearly as difficult or time-consuming as it was when my children were small, therefore many wives wonder what to do with their extra time. A mom of young children is a busy mom no matter what, but when they go off to school, she often wonders what to do with the rest of her life.

Now, I understand that economically, many mothers have to work. I know sometimes it's not even a question. It's something that must happen. That was the case for my own mother when she was struggling to raise my sister by herself. So I'm not talking to you if that's your situation.

But I do want to speak to the woman who does not need to work, but thinks she might like to. I have a guideline for you if you're that woman. I really feel this is from the Lord, because if you have your priorities right, your decisions will be right. You'll know just what you should do.

Here's the guideline: If God is first among all your priorities, and your home is second—meaning, you are able to keep up with all the Lord would have you do to keep a clean, peaceful, gracious home—then the addition of a career is fine.

But if you neglect the Lord or if you neglect your home in favor of a career, you will find yourself on a disastrous downward trail.

FULFILLMENT

Sometimes women will talk about their happiness and fulfillment, and make comments like, "I'm a much better mother if I'm fulfilled." Well, if your happiness and your fulfillment come first on your list, and your spiritual relationship and your family concerns come further down the list, your home will suffer.

No matter how uncomfortable that makes you feel, it's just the way it is—and it can't be changed. God's laws never change. If God tells you to be a keeper of the home and you won't do it, then nothing you try to find outside your home will give you the fulfillment you're looking for.

If you perceive your home and marriage to be a prison, then the atmosphere will be charged with resentment, irritability and hostility—and it will bear that fruit. The world's philosophy appeals to women because it says that she has a right to her feelings, her wants, and her needs, but the result is social chaos through the destruction of her home. And what causes that destruction? Selfishness.

It's been said that the opposite of love is not hate but indifference—a form of selfishness. It's choosing your way over what's best for your family. But when you're willing to lay down your life and defer your own ambitions and desires for a season, that choice will pay big dividends. Ultimately, it will yield the very fulfillment you're seeking.

RAISING YOUR CHILDREN

So many questions come to the surface when a woman with children contemplates having a career. First, who will care for your children if you work—and will they do it as well as you? I am convinced that no one could have raised my children as well as I could. Because they are my responsibility, God put a special love in my heart for my children.

Unless you're a mother without natural affection or you have resentment toward your children, you feel that special love too. Nobody will love them, pray for them or guide their little feet the way you will.

I told you right at the beginning that this would be an exhortative book—do you remember? I just feel so strongly about this that I have to urge you to consider these things. I can't help but wonder how many children's lives would be different today if their parents, particularly their mothers, were willing to make sacrifices for them—if they took time to teach them about God and about life ... if they were willing to go without certain material things in order to be there when the kids came home from school ... if they were more interested in their children's lives than in their own. You don't have children at home for long. You really don't. Remember that.

That leads to one final thought. Will you have regrets? Will you look back later and wonder if you had made the right choice? It's important to ask yourself this question, because if you add something as big as a career to your life, you can be sure other things will have to go by the wayside. Other things will be missed. Opportunities will be lost. All kinds of special moments in your child's life will happen outside of your presence. Time that you could have spent with them will be given to your job. Are you prepared for that?

Now, if you can work at an outside job and still take care of your family and your home—if your priorities are right and nothing is neglected—then I don't see anything wrong with having a job. But, if you still have small children at home, please wait. Those first five years in a child's life are so vital. It's your chance to program good things into them before they head off to school and discover other influences. You can do so much for the Lord and for His kingdom in those little lives during those precious years.

BE A BLESSING

My last encouragement to you is this: Be a blessing. If you will set yourself to being holy, wise, loving and obedient, you will be a blessing. You will not only bring joy to our Father's heart, but you'll also be a tremendous influence for Him in this world.

Our homes can be places where people find hope, healing and love. But only if the woman who keeps the home is one who has set her heart on reflecting God.

> Finally, all of you should be of one and the same mind united in spirit sympathizing with one another, loving each other as brethren of one household, compassionate and courteous (tenderhearted and humble-minded). Never return evil for evil or insult for insult (scolding, tongue-lashing, berating); but on the contrary, blessing, [praying for their welfare, happiness and protection and truly pitying and loving them] (1 Peter 3:8-9 *Amplified Bible*).

Father, search our hearts. If You find a struggle going on there, we ask that You open our eyes to see Your truth. If there is rebellion against being a keeper of the home, or being kindhearted, or postponing a career for the sake of little ones, we ask, Father, that You would be the Lord over all these decisions. Through our obedience to Your will, may we have a beautiful testimony to share with others.

And Lord, we thank You for the new beginnings You are always ready to give. We ask for a fresh start, and the anointing of Your Holy Spirit by which we will be able to honor You and reflect Your beauty and holiness to all we encounter.

We ask this in the precious name of Jesus. Amen.

CHAPTER

11

SHE IS AN INTERCESSOR

YOU CAN'T GO WRONG using Abigail as a role model for the kind of beautiful, godly woman you want to be—the kind of woman who reflects the Lord to others. Every time I read her story in 1 Samuel, chapter 25, I'm struck by what a wise woman and what a faithful intercessor she was for her family. She didn't have the Scriptures as we do now, of course. But she knew her Lord.

That's our desire too, isn't it? We want to know our Lord, because the days are getting darker and the world is getting increasingly desperate for Jesus. If we want to make Him known to others, we need to know Him ourselves. What better pursuit could there possibly be?

BEAUTY AND THE BEAST

Commentators like to entitle this particular Bible passage as "Beauty and the Beast." One look at 1 Samuel 25:3-11 substantiates this rather appropriate description of Abigail's husband as verse 3 begins with, "The name of the man was Nabal...."

Right from the get-go, we get a clue as to this man's character, because his name means "fool." Can you imagine anyone naming a baby "Fool"? I've heard some crazy names for babies, but this one is pretty bad. Bear this meaning in mind as we go through this passage. How would you like to be married to a fool? The answer, of course, is that you wouldn't.

But Abigail shows us that regardless of the kind of man you're married to, you have no excuse not to live for the Lord and to look for ways to bless and intercede for your family. If you live for Jesus, He will open doors for you no matter what your circumstances are. He'll make it possible for you to be the witness you ought to be, the daughter you should be, and the wife you need to be.

At the end of 1 Samuel 25:3, we get a bit more of a description of Nabal. "But the man was harsh and evil in his doings." The *King James Version* uses the word "churlish," which is found in no other place in the Bible. It means "cruel, hardhearted, and evil in his doings." How terrible to be married to a man who is cruel, hardhearted, and evil in his doings. Nabal was no Prince Charming.

GOOD UNDERSTANDING

Contrast the description of Nabal with that of Abigail.

> She was a woman of good understanding and beautiful appearance (1 Samuel 25:3).

I think when a woman has good understanding, she just naturally has a beautiful countenance. Something radiates through her that just gives her a touch of beauty. I have seen it over and over in the women in our church. Younger women, older women—it's a beauty that only God can give. It's the reflection of Christ, and no woman can have it apart from Him.

Many times when I've been at the market or somewhere else out in public, I'll see a woman and I'll say to Chuck, "I'll bet she's a Christian." When a person walks with Jesus, He shows on her face. So many times just after I've said that to Chuck, the woman will see us, and say, "Hi, Pastor Chuck." I love when I get that right.

Let's look at the rest of that passage together.

> When David heard in the wilderness that Nabal was shearing his sheep, David sent ten young men; and David said to the young men, "Go up to Carmel, go to Nabal, and greet him in my name. And thus you shall say to him who lives in prosperity: Peace be to you, peace be to your house, and peace to all that you have!
>
> "Now I have heard that you have shearers. Your shepherds were with us, and we did not hurt them, nor was there anything missing from them all the while they were in Carmel. Ask your young men, and they will tell you. Therefore let my young men find favor in your eyes, for we come on a feast day. Please give whatever comes to your hand to your servants and to your son David."
>
> So when David's young men came, they spoke to Nabal according to all these words in the name of David, and waited. Then Nabal answered David's servants, and said, "Who is David, and who is the son of Jesse? There are many servants nowadays who break away each one from his master. Shall I then take my bread and my water and my meat that I have killed for my shearers, and give it to men when I do not know where they are from?"

So David's young men turned on their heels and went back; and they came and told him all these words. Then David said to his men, "Every man gird on his sword." So every man girded on his sword, and David also girded on his sword. And about four hundred men went with David, and two hundred stayed with the supplies (1 Samuel 25:4-13).

Nabal proved his name by his actions. David and his men had been good to Nabal's shepherds when they had been out in the fields. Their presence had very likely prevented robbers from attacking Nabal's men and flocks, which was a common problem in those days. Had they not been a protective barrier, Nabal's profit could have been considerably smaller.

So what they asked of Nabal was not unreasonable. Someone with any integrity or hospitality at all would have been happy to provide food for David and his men. But Nabal was not such a man.

First Samuel 25 goes on to tell us that one of Nabal's young men, who overheard the conversation between his master and David's messenger, went to Abigail and warned her of what had happened.

The men were very good to us, and we were not hurt, nor did we miss anything as long as we accompanied them, when we were in the fields. They were a wall to us both by night and day, all the time we were with them keeping the sheep (1 Samuel 25:15-16).

ALERT TO DANGER

Abigail was smart enough to recognize her household was in danger. Some women do not seem to have this kind of awareness. Whether they don't see it or they don't want to see it, some women seem to sit by while trouble invades their home.

My kids used to tease me because they knew I would go into their rooms and "straighten up" their drawers. While I was in there cleaning up, I might happen to glance around to make sure there was nothing hidden that would be dangerous to them. Those were crazy days at our church because we had so many young people coming in. Not everyone who came to Calvary Chapel was there because they wanted to give themselves to Jesus. Some tried to slip in and mingle with the group because they thought it would be an easy place to sell drugs.

I wanted to be observant. They understood why I was doing it. So they'd tease me. "Isn't she a dear mommy to put our socks away for us?" But I was watching out for them.

Jeff had one friend who was a consummate liar. I had never met anybody like him in my life. One day as he was rattling on about some story, I called him on it. "Now, you know that's not true," I said. "You don't say those things to your mom, do you?"

"Yeah, I do," he said. "She believes everything I say."

I stood looking at him thinking, *I'm going to call her!* I didn't, but maybe I should have. We moms have to be on the alert. The stakes are just too high.

Back then I was determined by God's grace to keep my eyes on my children and know as much about their lives as I could. I even had my friends praying for them. We had a group of women at church who prayed our kids would not get entrapped by drugs.

You know, it's as dangerous for a Christian kid as it is for a worldly kid—Christian kids can be even bigger targets. Satan is working overtime to get at our children. You have to be like Abigail. You have to be alert to the things going on around you and watch for signs of danger.

Abigail didn't ignore the information the young man brought to her. The Word tells us,

Then Abigail made haste and took two hundred loaves of bread, two skins of wine, five sheep already dressed, five measures of roasted grain, one hundred clusters of raisins, and two hundred cakes of figs, and loaded them on donkeys (1 Samuel 25:18).

Sometimes we need to make haste. The temptation might be to sit back and wait, but you have to resist that temptation when danger is coming toward your household.

PRACTICAL WISDOM

We see further proof of Abigail's wisdom in the preparations she made to take to David. What do men love? Food! I remember when I was a young wife and I attended a Christian seminar. The speaker instructed all the wives, "When your husband comes home, you should always have something on the stove that smells good."

Men just love that. Chuck may never notice when I'm wearing perfume, but he notices right away if something's cooking when he walks through the front door. A wise woman has food available. And Abigail was a wise woman.

David was infuriated by Nabal's insult. We read,

Now David had said, "Surely in vain I have protected all that this fellow has in the wilderness, so that nothing was missed of all that belongs to him. And he has repaid me evil for good. May God do so, and more also, to the enemies of David, if I leave one male of all who belong to him by morning light" (1 Samuel 25:21-22).

David was full of wrath at this point. But Proverbs 15:1 tells us that, "A gentle answer turns away wrath."

Abigail must have known this, because she had the wisdom to approach David with humility and gentleness.

We read,

> Now when Abigail saw David, she hastened to dismount from the donkey, fell on her face before David, and bowed down to the ground. So she fell at his feet and said: "On me, my lord, on me let this iniquity be! And please let your maidservant speak in your ears, and hear the words of your maidservant" (1 Samuel 25:23-24).

STAND IN THE GAP

Incredibly, Abigail took responsibility for everything that had happened. She acted as an intercessor for her household, willing to stand in the gap to protect them. To save her house, she reasoned with David.

> "Please, let not my lord regard this scoundrel Nabal. For as his name is, so is he: Nabal is his name, and folly is with him! But I, your maidservant, did not see the young men of my lord whom you sent. Now therefore, my lord, as the LORD lives and as your soul lives, since the LORD has held you back from coming to bloodshed and from avenging yourself with your own hand, now then, let your enemies and those who seek harm for my lord be as Nabal.

> "And now this present which your maidservant has brought to my lord, let it be given to the young men who follow my lord. Please forgive the trespass of your maidservant. For the LORD will certainly make for my lord an enduring house, because my lord fights the battles of the LORD, and evil is not found in you throughout your days.

> "Yet a man has risen to pursue you and seek your life, but the life of my lord shall be bound in the bundle of the living with the LORD your God; and the lives of your enemies He shall sling out, as from the pocket of a sling.

> "And it shall come to pass, when the LORD has done for my lord according to all the good that He has spoken concerning you, and has appointed you ruler over Israel, that this will be no grief to you, nor offense of heart

to my lord, either that you have shed blood without cause, or that my lord has avenged himself. But when the LORD has dealt well with my lord, then remember your maidservant" (1 Samuel 25:25-31).

KNOWLEDGE OF THE LORD

What strikes me when I read this passage is Abigail's knowledge of the Lord. The word "lord" is scattered throughout her speech as she's using that word to address David. But seven times she uses "LORD," meaning God. She knew Him. She knew Him well enough that she understood His heart and His character.

I love the beautiful expression she used in verse 29 when she said,

> But the life of my lord shall be bound in the bundle of the living with the LORD your God.

What a lovely way to say that our lives are in the hands of God! Abigail knew that no one can touch us or take us out of His hands. That deserves a "Praise the Lord!" or an "Amen!"

As I said, Abigail didn't have the Scriptures like we have them today. But that didn't stop her from accepting and believing everything she did manage to learn. She was devoted to God. When you think of what we have at our fingertips today—books, radio broadcasts, internet podcasts, dozens of Bible translations—you realize there's no excuse for not being spiritually fed in this day and age.

We shouldn't take for granted all that is available to us, nor should we excuse negligence. We must take every opportunity to just breathe in His presence and His power and His Word.

I like to leave my Bible on my bed in the morning. Sometimes if I am running back up to my room for a few minutes, I'll open my Bible and ask, "What do You want to say to me, Lord?" Now, sometimes I get funny

Scriptures, so I'm not advising this as your sole source of devotional reading. But just as a quick extra feeding on the Word, it works fine. I usually flip through until I find one that would be good to meditate on until the next time I run upstairs. And do you know what that does? It takes all the worry and pressure out of my mind and puts the Word of God in there instead. This is how we are strengthened.

SEEK GOD'S PROTECTION

Abigail was a woman who knew the Lord well enough that she was able to give a prophetic exhortation to David—one that David recognized. As she was speaking, David realized God was speaking to him through her.

> Then David said to Abigail, "Blessed is the LORD God of Israel, who sent you this day to meet me! And blessed is your advice and blessed are you, because you have kept me this day from coming to bloodshed and from avenging myself with my own hand. For indeed, as the LORD God of Israel lives, who has kept me back from hurting you, unless you had hastened and come to meet me, surely by morning light no males would have been left to Nabal!" (1 Samuel 25:32-34).

How precious that David—this wonderful man of God—wasn't so high and mighty or untouchable that he couldn't receive from this gifted woman. Abigail's prophecy spoke of the time when he would be king. She warned him of the grief he would suffer if he had bloodshed on his hands.

And David listened, because God was in her counsel. David was spared that grief because Abigail was willing to put her own life on the line to counsel him. Oh, I want to be a woman of wise counsel. Don't you?

Abigail succeeded. She interceded for her family and averted a disaster. She kept her household safe. Is your household safe today because of your intercession? Do you call out to God when you see danger approaching your home?

Beloved sister, it is not too late to begin to be an Abigail. Start today by getting on your knees and seeking God's protection over your home and your loved ones. In the end, your testimony can be as precious as that of Abigail.

WAIT FOR DELIVERANCE

The conclusion to this situation is truly amazing. We read that, "The LORD struck Nabal, and he died" (1 Samuel 25:38). God didn't leave Abigail in that awful place. She didn't have to act on her own behalf, she didn't have to fight Nabal. She simply waited for deliverance and it came.

God will always care for the one who puts her trust in Him. He'll remove you from the situation or He'll give you the strength and the courage to endure it. God will always protect the ones who trust in Him and He will intervene on your behalf.

After Nabal died, word reached David of what had happened. First he praised God for keeping him from committing that evil act, and then he sent word to Abigail asking her to be his wife. Listen to the surprising thing Abigail did upon hearing those words.

> Then she arose, bowed her face to the earth, and said, "Here is your maidservant, a servant to wash the feet of the servants of my lord" (1 Samuel 25:41).

Now, if somebody came to you and said, "You're going to be the king's wife," would you have reacted like this? Would I? Probably not. For most of us, our very first response would be, "What shall I wear?"

HUMILITY

We need the humility of Abigail. Because the truth is, every one of us who has been adopted into God's family truly is the bride of the King. We're the bride of Christ (Revelation 21:9).

God doesn't always call us to literally wash the feet of others. Sometimes He does. But more often, we're called to wash feet in the spiritual sense by loving others, by going beyond what's comfortable and what we feel we have time for.

The night before Jesus was to be crucified—knowing all things—Jesus took the time for His friends and served them. He humbled Himself to teach them one last lesson on how to love others.

In the gospel of John we read,

> So when He (Jesus) had washed their feet, taken His garments, and sat down again, He said to them, "Do you know what I have done to you? You call Me Teacher and Lord, and you say well, for so I am.
>
> If I then, your Lord and Teacher, have washed your feet, you also ought to wash one another's feet. For I have given you an example, that you should do as I have done to you. Most assuredly, I say to you, a servant is not greater than his master; nor is he who is sent greater than he who sent him. If you know these things, blessed are you if you do them (John 13:12-17).

From this account, we can clearly see how Abigail reflected God. The same humility and selflessness that was in Abigail needs to be in us. So the question to ask yourself is: Are you willing to wash feet? Will you take the time?

LOVING OTHERS

Maybe you're like me and you have certain people in your life who demand a lot of your time. Now and then I've had those situations. Years ago, one particular lady used to call me every week. I must confess that when I would answer the phone and find it was her, my initial reaction was usually a prayer of desperation. "Oh, Father, I have so much to do today! Please—I just can't do this."

But then God would speak to my heart. He'd say, "Love will do it. Don't think of yourself—think of her. I'll make up the time for you." And He would. He's never failed me in that.

This lady was very sad and lonely. She was calling because she knew she needed prayer. She wasn't looking for me to fix her problems. She just wanted someone to listen and to pray with her—and I needed to be tested. Would I wash her feet? Would I love her? Would I take the time?

I've often wondered if, when I get to heaven, I might find out that those times I loved her by listening and praying with her were the finest ministry I ever did.

Spend some time this week meditating on Abigail's example. She was a woman of good understanding and humility. She was a woman devoted to God and filled with the knowledge of the Lord. And all those traits came together to help her intercede for her family at a critical time. What might be coming in your life? What are you doing right now to prepare yourself to be an intercessor?

Father, thank You for giving us Abigail's story. We would have missed her great example had You not done so. But You included her story that we might be touched and moved to ask You for those same traits. Help her example not to fade from the pages of our minds, our hearts, or our spirits.

Lord, in those times when we're tempted to do our own will or to be selfish, or those times when we are drawn toward complacency instead of action, may we remember the very great need for humility and intercession. Help us to reflect Your love to others.

In Jesus' name we ask. Amen.

12

SHE NURTURES THE YOUNG

WHEN IT COMES TO CHILDREN and the influence we, as adults, have on them, every circumstance is different. Your children might be very small or they might be fully grown. Maybe you're a grandmother like me and you're blessed to be able to spend a lot of time with your grandchildren. Maybe you're a guardian for a child, filling in for the role of a mother. Or maybe you do not have children of your own, but you do care for children through your job or through your ministry.

Regardless of your circumstance, if you're a woman, God has given you nurturing abilities. And those abilities are to be used generously on the children under your influence.

It seems Chuck and I are always being asked advice about child rearing. Before we were parents ourselves, we could give tons of advice on how to raise children. But since having them, we have learned that we can only tell you very few things.

What I do know, I'm happy to share with you, because I've seen these principles proven over and over again. I pray you'll take them to heart, because there's something quite beautiful about watching a godly woman nurturing little ones for Jesus.

The most important advice I can give you really encapsulates all of them. If you do this one thing first, the rest will flow from that. And it's this: Love the children God has entrusted to you. Love them, love them, love them. You really can't overdo this. You cannot give them too much. If you just pour love on children for twenty-four hours a day, seven days a week, it still won't be too much. Children thrive under love as a plant does in the sun. This is not limited to small children either. They need love at all stages.

Here are some practical ways to express your love:

1. PRAY FOR THEM

When you love someone, you want to ask God's blessing and His protection on that person, don't you? This is such an easy way to show your children how much they mean to you—and it's so important to bathe your children in prayer, especially in these dark days.

You start when they are first placed in your arms and continue right on after that. When my children began going to school, I always prayed with them in the morning before they headed out. Always.

Sometimes one of my kids would try to evade it and slip out the door. But as that one was going down the sidewalk, I'd open the door and say,

"May the Lord bless you this day and keep you in His love and in His will and keep you in obedience."

I'd get a mumbled "Thanks, Mom" back. But now that they're all grown, they've told me how much they relied on those prayers throughout their day at school. And it doesn't stop there. Your children will always need your prayers.

If you're a woman who does not have children of your own, but you love and nurture the children of others, prayer is one of the greatest gifts you can give them. And how it will bless the heart of the Lord to see your love reflected through your prayers on their behalf.

2. TEACH THEM THE FEAR AND ADMONITION OF GOD

Look for opportunities to plant seeds in the children God has given you influence over. Have devotions with them. Let them hear you praying. Let them see you reading your Bible.

When our granddaughter, Kristyn, was very little, she was so used to seeing our Bibles that she knew what they were. She'd see one of our Bibles sitting on the counter or the table and she'd point and say, "Bible!" It was one of her first words, and we were so blessed by it.

Obviously, one of the best things you can do is to take your children to Sunday school where they can sing songs and hear Bible stories. Not only do they need the stimulation of other children, it's also good for them to be around other adults who love the Lord.

If this isn't something you've been doing with your children or your grandchildren, start now. Today is a good day to begin building them up in the ways of the Lord. It's never too late to start.

3. LAUGH WITH THEM

Don't children say the funniest things? You just can't help but laugh at some of the things that come out of their mouths. Kids are a lot of work and they're a lot of heartache, but they're also a lot of fun.

Enjoy your children. Have a sense of humor with them. Learn how to make up little games together. One thing I always liked to do with my grandchildren was to pick them up and say, "I need love." They knew to bend their little heads over and let me kiss their cheeks. That was just something we did together. You can create your own special little games with your children and grandchildren. They'll love it, and they'll never forget it.

4. OPEN UP THE WORLD TO THEM

Children are just naturally curious—especially in those early toddler years. They need to be able to discover their environment to satisfy that curiosity. The brightest children are often the ones who ask the most questions—the "whys" of the world. "Why is sand wet when it's near the beach?" and "Why is the sky blue?"

Take the time to answer the questions your little ones ask. Talk *to* them, not around them. Include them in your conversations with others, no matter how young they are. I believe in talking to babies right from the first moment they arrive. "Hi, beautiful baby! Do you know Jesus is your Savior?"

Along with talking to them early, make sure you read to them. This is a wonderful way to open up the world. They won't understand you at first, but they'll listen. They'll learn to pick out words and they'll learn to love reading if you'll just take the time to introduce them to books from the earliest age. When they get old enough to interact with the story, ask them questions about what you've read together. Sometimes their responses are really funny.

When she was two, Cheryl really liked the story of *Goldilocks and the Three Bears*, so we read it to her all the time. One morning she refused to eat her eggs, so we reminded her about Goldilocks.

"Remember Papa Bear and Mama Bear and Baby Bear? They all had their cereal and they all ate it … Goldilocks ate it all up. Why don't you be like Goldilocks and eat your eggs all up? Now, what did Goldilocks do with her cereal?"

Cheryl said, "Thew it in the twashcan."

One of the best pieces of parenting advice I ever heard was, "Strew pretty things in your child's path." What this means is we should purposely surround them with beauty. Children are interested in beautiful things. Why put every pretty thing up out of reach?

I let my children (and now my grandchildren) handle some of my ceramic pieces. So far, nothing has gotten broken. Ceramics are interesting to small children. They like the smoothness, the color, and the shine. Why deprive them of a chance to touch something so beautiful?

Hang pictures in your child's room. You can frame a poster or find some artwork they would enjoy, or maybe put up some Bible verses written in calligraphy or in your nicest handwriting. I put a lot of verses on the walls of my children's bedrooms.

I think they learned a lot of Scriptures just because they had so much time to stare at them. I don't think there was any conscious effort at all. It's not hard to memorize God's Word when it's hanging above your bed where you can see it all the time.

Take your child on lots of walks and let them investigate the things they see along the way. Don't pick the neighbor's flowers, of course, but if you happen to come upon something wild growing along the way, don't stop your little one from picking and smelling a flower. They're curious about the color and texture of growing things. Watch them closely—but don't deprive them of touching and exploring such things.

Another way to open the world for your child is to give them freedom to play. When we first began having children, Chuck told me that we were not to have a "no-no house." Do you know what that is? That's a house where everything is off-limits to the child. Everything is a big no-no for them. So we made sure the children were free to play and explore.

Now that we have grandchildren and our home is roomier, we've set the family room aside for this. It has a big toy box and an older couch and a couple of chairs that can't be hurt. Our grandkids have all kinds of toys, including a train track to play with in there. That room is always a little bit upside down because it belongs to the kids, but that's okay. They can touch anything they want in that room.

I don't want to leave you with the impression that I've always been easy-going about such things. I've had to learn. But God has been faithful to bring every lesson I needed to help me let go in this area.

BE LONGSUFFERING

Many years back, the hippies made a banner for me that listed the fruit of the Spirit. It read:

> The fruit of the Spirit is love, joy, peace, longsuffering, kindness, goodness, faithfulness, gentleness, self-control (Galatians 5:22-23).

We hung it right next to the door between the living room and the kitchen. Of course, "longsuffering" was the longest word on it and it was at eye-level for me, so every time I walked through the doorway, that word "longsuffering" would catch my eye. Truthfully, I would rather have fixed my gaze on "love" or "joy" or "peace," but "longsuffering" was the one that caught my attention every time.

I remember one Christmas our boys began wrestling after we'd opened all our presents. They weren't really fighting as if to hurt one another, they were just playing around and duking it out the way boys do. We were all in the living room watching the chaos, and Chuck was loving it, but I could hear them crunching presents with their feet and I started saying, "No, no, no!" The girls were screaming at the boys about their presents being ruined and Chuck was laughing and no one could even hear me in all that commotion.

So I thought, *I can't take this one more minute.* I walked into the kitchen to go start the dinner preparation, and as I went through the doorway, that word was staring at me. "Longsuffering." Longsuffering means to have patience with people and to let your love come through. So I thought, *Oh, well, all those presents are going to burn anyway.* Somehow, the Lord mellowed me out. I quit worrying about it. And you know what? Just as soon as I got my attitude right, they quit wrestling around. I passed the test. It's not always easy, but we will get better at being patient and easygoing and longsuffering if we keep trying.

BE FLEXIBLE

So be flexible and patient with your children. And be spontaneous. Grab a loaf of bread and head to the park to feed the ducks. Visit the zoo or a children's museum. Make a play date with other children so they get lots of social interaction.

Buy some craft supplies and let them make a mess at the kitchen table. Are you getting the idea? Do whatever you can to stimulate your child's interests, open their horizons, and give them opportunities to satisfy their curiosity.

One last thought about this suggestion. If you're purposeful about these things, and you truly want to help your child discover his or her world, you need to be prepared for some interruptions. Permit these to happen. I'm not suggesting that you don't teach your child proper manners, but I am saying that you should never shut your child down when he comes to you with a question.

For example, if you're sitting and reading the Bible and your child comes in with a question, don't say, "Out! I am reading the Word of God." That kind of response really doesn't teach your child something wonderful about God, does it? Sometimes you have to put your Bible down for a moment and let them know how important they are to you.

5. EXPRESS YOUR DELIGHT IN THEM

I remember our little Kristyn when she was just a tiny girl and she had learned to wink while we were away at a pastors' conference. Well, the moment we got home we asked her to wink for us. And every time she did it, Grandma and Grandpa would say, "Ah, you adorable little thing." She'd just smile, as if to say that she knew how cute she was.

Children need to know you're delighted with them. They need it! When was the last time you told your toddler or your teenager or even your adult child, "You mean so much to me. How did I get so blessed to have a child like you?"

6. GUIDE AND CORRECT THEM

Discipline is an important part of loving your children, but discipline does not mean beating them. It has broken my heart so many times to be walking through the store and to see a mother haul off and hit her little child. If anything makes me feel violent myself, it's witnessing that.

You know, those little legs have to take three steps to keep up with one of ours. They need patience from their mamas. And if you'll pardon me for saying this so bluntly, any dumb woman can hit her child. It takes restraint, tenderness and creativity to correct their behavior in a way that will lovingly guide them.

I do believe in spanking children when they need it, but I also believe that should be your very last resort, and only for the most serious sort of offenses. I also feel strongly that parents should not be slapping their child's hand every time they get into something they shouldn't. What will that child think of the world? What kind of parents will they be themselves if that's what's modeled to them?

Instead of slapping your child's hand when they're drawn to something they shouldn't touch, try distracting them instead. I remember Chuck talking about this in a sermon once. He pointed out that God doesn't slap us every time we do something we shouldn't. Instead, He often distracts us by bringing along something that's even more interesting or more wonderful than the thing we're tempted by.

Try doing this with your child as much as possible, especially when they're young. Distract them from what they're doing. You can gently say, "No, no." Sometimes it might be necessary to give them a little tap on the hand if they persist in what they're doing, but don't do this often. Restrain yourself as much as possible.

If you withhold firm, loving discipline from your child, you actually hurt them in the long run. Good parents help their children learn how to discipline themselves and control their emotions. Remember, discipline is not punishment. It is training.

7. PRAISE THEM

You can't go wrong by pouring out praise and encouragement on your children. Too often, though, we're quick with disapproval and stingy with approval. As I mentioned in an earlier chapter, I read a study once that concluded parents gave six disapproving comments for every one praise.

That's six times more criticism than encouragement! I wouldn't flourish much under that, would you? None of us really blossom under criticism. Praise, on the other hand, can open up a child and encourage them to keep moving forward. Bless the children in your life with some praise today. You'll be blessed right back.

8. HONOR THEIR INDIVIDUALITY

Our son, Jeff, was way ahead of his time when it came to wearing his hair long. His hair always grew fast, and nothing we did could hold it back. It looked adorable on him and he really liked it long. So I finally decided, Why fight it? Since he liked it that much, we let him keep it long. Actually, our whole family thought it looked adorable on him.

But one day at church, a woman came up to Jeff and said, "You know, your mother ought to get you a haircut."

Oh, dear, I thought. I was so embarrassed. So I said, "Honey, I guess we better get you a haircut."

But Jeff didn't want a haircut. He said, "Mom, I want to wear it this way."

I had to make a choice. I could either give Jeff the freedom to express himself or I could protect my pride. So I sacrificed my pride, let Jeff keep his long hair, and tried to avoid that woman at church.

You need God's wisdom on these matters. Not every choice our children want to make is a safe or healthy choice. But when it's not dangerous or ungodly, and the struggle is really between your preference and your child's preference, ask the Lord to give you the graciousness to step aside and give your child some freedom. It's so important that we learn to choose our battles carefully. Not everything has to go the way we would prefer it.

PUT AWAY WORRY

Parenting brings with it a lot of fears. You worry when they're little, you worry when they go to school, you worry when they start to drive, and you worry when they head out on their own. Worry just seems to be a natural part of parenting. But God would have us put away that worry and depend on Him.

Isaiah 41:10 is a verse that has brought me tremendous comfort over the years. It's a verse I've learned to apply to my parenting.

Through Isaiah, God tells us in this passage,

> Fear not, for I am with you; be not dismayed, for I am your God. I will strengthen you, yes, I will help you, I will uphold you with My righteous right hand.

Some years ago we lived in an area with busy traffic. Day and night, you could hear sirens whizzing by the neighborhood—sirens, sirens, sirens, nonstop. Well, during the time we lived there, Chuck was terribly busy at the church. It was right during the explosion of the Jesus Movement when all the hippies were coming to Jesus.

So I had the pure joy and fun of being with my children while they learned to drive. I got all those first few months of rides with them—over hedges and into fences, and one time almost over the bluff. I came close to losing my life several times, but God protected me.

Every Sunday morning when Chuck Jr. was learning to drive, the whole family (except for Chuck) would be in the car on the way to church, and we'd get in a fight—every single Sunday.

One of the kids would get scared—usually it was Jeff—and he'd start stomping on the imaginary brake in front of his seat. Janette would say, "Chuck, you're going through that stop sign!" And he'd say, "Well, there's nobody coming either way," as he sailed on through it. Oh, I tell you, it was craziness, that's what it was.

DEPEND ON GOD'S PROMISES

So when Chuck Jr. or Janette was out with my car and I'd hear a siren, I would become filled with fear. My heart would constrict and I'd get that fluttery, butterfly feeling in my stomach. This went on for weeks and weeks and weeks.

Finally, one day when the kids were out, I heard another siren going down the street, and I thought, *I can't take this any longer. I just can't.* So I looked at that verse in Isaiah 41 and I personalized it. I added just a little at the end so that it said, "Fear not, for I am with you—and I am with your children."

Then I prayed, "All right, Lord, from this day on, I will never be fearful again. When I hear a siren and our kids are out in the car, I'm going to remember that You're watching over them. I'll know they're going to be okay."

Do you realize when you make a declaration that you're going to believe in and depend upon God's promises, almost immediately Satan tries to shatter that confidence?

The very next day, Chuck had a day off. As is usually the case, even though it was his day off, we had been down at the church working on something. On the way home, I asked him if we could stop at the market to pick up something for dinner.

The problem was, I wasn't really dressed appropriately for going to the market. I was dressed for working down at the church cleaning or painting or whatever it was I'd been doing. So I said, "Honey, would you mind running in?"

He said he would, of course, and we stopped at a little market not too far from our house. So while I was sitting in the car, I heard sirens start up from a fire station that was just a few blocks up from the market. And I thought, *Isn't it lovely not to be fearful when I hear a siren?*

But as the fire trucks came by the market, I heard this loud blast from the radio, and this voice said, "Fire at 729 St. James Road." That was the house right next door to ours!

I'd left Cheryl home with a bunch of friends playing in the backyard. Of course, all my peaceful thoughts fled. I thought, *There's a fire! There's a fire! Where's Chuck?* But I couldn't wait for him. I started the car and drove off, stranding him there at the market.

I arrived home to see a huge fire in the yard next door—right up close to our back fence and lots of fire engines, people running around and all the neighbors standing there gawking.

I first ran out back to check on the children, and when I could see they were all right, I asked someone what had happened. Apparently, the neighbor had been chopping down a tree and it hit an electrical wire, which sparked and caught the tree on fire.

Back at the market, Chuck came out with two big bags of groceries. He told me later he stood there a minute thinking, *Where's my wife? What did I say?* He couldn't figure out what in the world he had done to make me leave.

As we were all standing around watching the firemen handle the fire hoses and all the commotion, I suddenly remembered Chuck. I said to Janette, "Oh, I left Daddy at the market."

"You did what?" So she went back and got her daddy.

RELY ON GOD'S WORD

When you decide to depend on God's promises, you will be tested. It just happens. Satan will batter at the door of your heart to try to destroy your confidence and fill you with fear. Stand firm! Fear never purchased anything for us, did it? It gave us nothing except anxiety, stress, high blood pressure and heart attacks. So God tells us to "fear not." He reminds us that He is right there with us. When the realization comes that the Creator of the universe is with you, fear and dismay vanish.

If you're full of fear today, you need to begin relying on God's Word. Get alone and say out loud to Him, "God, You promised You would be with me. You've told me not to be fearful. So I'm going to give You all my worries and fearful thoughts and I'm going to trust what You said in Your Word. I'm going to believe that You're with me and my children." Then picture the arms of Jesus surrounding your loved ones and guiding the feet of your children.

I pray that whoever you are to the little ones in your life—mother, aunt, grandmother, or teacher—God gives you wisdom and patience and an endless supply of love. May He bless you as you minister to His precious children.

Father, what would we do without You? We rejoice in the promises of Your Word and in the knowledge that whatever task You put before us, You always supply the tools we need to accomplish it.

I pray, Lord, that You will equip the woman reading this book to minister Your love to the children in her life. Make her aware of how great this privilege is. Strengthen her and anoint her for this nurturing task, that she would be a bright example of Your love to all who see her.

We pray this in Jesus' name. Amen.

CHAPTER

13

SHE INSPIRES OTHERS

THE BOOK OF JUDGES IS one of the saddest accounts of Israel's history in the entire Bible. It's a story filled with idolatry, sin, and an almost persistent rejection of God's laws.

Time after time, Israel would abandon the ways of the Lord in order to follow the pagan practices around them.

Then, after they'd wallowed in all that filth for a while, God would bring someone along to correct them. After that correction did its work and they finally cried out to God, He would deliver them—and then the cycle would start all over again.

As we read in Judges 2:16-19,

> Nevertheless, the LORD raised up judges who delivered them out of the hand of those who plundered them. Yet they would not listen to their judges, but they played the harlot with other gods, and bowed down to them. They turned quickly from the way in which their fathers walked, in obeying the commandments of the LORD; they did not do so.
>
> And when the LORD raised up judges for them, the LORD was with the judge and delivered them out of the hand of their enemies all the days of the judge; for the LORD was moved to pity by their groaning because of those who oppressed them and harassed them.
>
> And it came to pass, when the judge was dead, that they reverted and behaved more corruptly than their fathers, by following other gods, to serve them and bow down to them.

Israel simply would not renounce their idolatry. Every time they had an opportunity to turn back to pagan idols, they did so.

It's easy for us to look at that time in history and think, *I'd never turn to idolatry*, but that's just because we don't recognize it in our own culture. There's a great deal of idolatry in our age. Maybe we don't fix little bowls of rice to offer to our idols, and we don't go to the butcher shop and see a sign advertising "Meats formerly offered up to idols."

But there's idolatry everywhere around us. Our culture is in as grave a state as Israel was during the time of the judges. Our world needs men and women who will stand up against idolatry and influence the lost back to God.

GOD'S FRIEND

In the midst of the darkness of that time, God raised up a woman by the name of Deborah (Judges 4:4). We don't know a lot about her. We know that she was married to a man by the name of Lapidoth.

We don't know Deborah's age, her height, her weight—we don't know whether she was beautiful or plain. None of those details mattered enough to God to record in His Word. Isn't that interesting?

It makes us wonder, *What would I want recorded about me?* I think so often we worry about all the wrong things. We look at our driver's license and think, *I've gained twenty pounds since that picture was taken.*

That was my thought when it was almost time for my new passport several years ago. I thought, *Why did I let myself gain these twenty pounds? Everyone is going to see that new passport!* It seems like we worry so much more about what we look like than what we act like. But God is not concerned with those outer details.

STIRRED TO ACTION

So we don't know much about Deborah's physical appearance. But we do know that Deborah was a close friend of God and that she reflected the heart of God, because she was chosen to be a judge in Israel. She ministered for the Lord by sitting under a palm tree and listening to the disputes and complaints of the children of Israel.

In my own life, the calls I receive from hurting people frequently drive me to prayer and to action. So often when I see the destructive works of Satan in the lives of these believers, it grieves me so much that I have to cry out for their deliverance. I think that may have been what happened to Deborah. Day after day the people came to her and poured out their hearts about the oppression they suffered under Jabin, the Canaanite king. I think that after she'd heard enough, God stirred her to action.

Judges 4:6 tells us that one day Deborah called Barak, son of Abinoam, who was one of the leaders of Israel. After hearing so many complaints from the people, it would have been easy for Deborah to just jump all over Barak and his soldiers.

She could have said, "You weak-kneed, spineless men of Israel, what in the world is wrong with you? You wimps. You gutless wonders. Jabin's army is out there, and you won't do a thing about it. Twenty years we've been living under his oppression, and I seem to be the only one who cares."

AN ENCOURAGER

But that's not what Deborah said. Instead, she encouraged him.

> Has not the LORD God of Israel commanded, "Go and deploy troops at Mount Tabor; take with you ten thousand men of the sons of Naphtali and of the sons of Zebulun; and against you I will deploy Sisera, the commander of Jabin's army, with his chariots and his multitude at the River Kishon; and I will deliver him into your hand"? (Judges 4:6-7).

Not only did Deborah give Barak the strategy for battle, she also told him the outcome. "Barak, I've heard from God. I'm just telling you what He said to do, and what He promised to do on your behalf. There is great anointing on you, Barak. Go forth."

But Barak didn't burst forth with great enthusiasm. He said in Judges 4:8, "If you will go with me, then I will go; but if you will not go with me, I will not go!" That's not exactly something that would build great confidence in you, is it? Still, Deborah's prophecy encouraged Barak to enlist 10,000 men and go out against Jabin's army (Judges 4:14). She inspired him to move out and act for God.

BREATHE LIFE INTO OTHERS

The word "inspire" means to affect, guide, or arouse by divine influence; to breathe life into.

Let me ask you this: Do you breathe life into the men in your life? Are you a woman who inspires men for God? Or are you so interested in the body beautiful that when you come across a desirable man someplace, you think, *Oh, I hope my hair and makeup look all right. I hope my figure is okay.* Is that the kind of inspiration you are concerned with, or do you really want to inspire men towards God?

You might think, *Oh, Kay, you're over the hill. You're a grandmother. Of course you want to inspire men for God—what else?* But I want you to know that the earnest desire of my heart since I met my Lord Jesus Christ and began to grow in Him has been to inspire men towards God. That should be the desire of every Christian woman, regardless of her age.

Certainly, every married woman should learn to inspire her husband. Back when I was a young romantic, maybe eighteen or nineteen, I thought Elizabeth Barrett Browning's poem that began, "How do I love thee? Let me count the ways ..." [19] was so romantic and beautiful that I memorized the whole thing, and I used to say it to whomever I was going with at the time. We're foolish at that age, aren't we? Some of us kept falling in and out of love. I did, until I met *the one.* At any rate, I used the poem a lot. But you know, after I got married, I didn't use it very much.

Have you ever said to your husband, "How do I love thee? Let me count the ways"? "I love you because of this ... I love you because of that." Oh, that inspires him. Do you know that is one of the deepest needs your husband has to hear from you? Many great men today are great because a woman under God inspired them.

You can also inspire him right into hell. You can make his life such a miserable mess through nagging, discontentment and constant criticism that you push him right into the Devil's territory. It's in your hands. Do you want to be an inspiration? And I don't mean just to your husband. Do you want to be an inspiration to other men, to women, to your children or your grandchildren?

BE A GODLY INFLUENCE

So how do we become the kind of woman who encourages, inspires, and influences others? If you're married, you might be saying, "My husband? I could inspire a rock quicker. Once that ball game is on, I can't even get his attention."

Well, in and of yourself you probably can't. But God can create something out of nothing. He can make you a godly influence to your husband. I've seen it happen. If you're single, He can make you an inspiration to every man you meet.

Years ago we had a beautiful girl in the church office whose name, interestingly enough, was Deborah. Every man who came across her path went away breathless. She was physically beautiful, but that really had nothing to do with it. It was the Spirit of the Lord shining through her that drew people. No matter how stressed I was, if I called the church office and Deborah answered, a calming sweetness would come over me.

Chuck's Aunt Lois fell and broke her shoulder one day. He happened to be in Indonesia at the time, so the nurse called and told me about the injury. I was on my way to a retreat planning meeting which several of our pastors' wives had flown in to attend. I couldn't miss that meeting, so I called around and tried to get somebody in the family to get to the hospital. I was finally able to round up a few.

I then called the church office and Deborah answered the phone. I explained the situation and relayed to her what the nurse had told me, which was that Aunt Lois would improve if she had lots of visitors. I said, "Would you ask around and see if some of the pastors would go up to the hospital to see her?" Deborah did. She told the pastors. But you know who went right away? Deborah. And you know the report? She called and said, "Oh Kay, I had the most glorious time with Aunt Lois."

Now, Aunt Lois was someone whom we had tried and tried to invite to church, but she never visited. And I honestly can't remember ever having had a glorious time with her, I'm sorry to say. But somehow, Deborah brought that out in her.

After my meeting, when I was able to go to the hospital, I walked into the room and saw a girl I had never met before, arranging carnations in a vase for Aunt Lois. Her name was Carolyn and she was Deborah's roommate. Oh, the sweet inspiration of Deborah!

Women need this quality. We want to reflect God to the world and we want to be His influence wherever we go. We want to inspire everyone He brings across our path. Don't you want that? We can choose to live a discontented, unhappy, miserable life. Or we can ask God to give us that meek and gentle spirit that's such a delight to Him, and create in us a sweetness and a peaceableness that inspires others toward Him.

CREDIBILITY

If you're looking at yourself and you're thinking, *That's not me. I'm not a godly influence to anybody*, it may be because you have not established credibility in the Christian circle or in the world. Maybe you vacillate too much. The people who are watching your life see you compromising with the world one day and trying to talk about spiritual things the next.

But if you are to influence men for righteousness, godliness and holiness, and cause them to stand up as soldiers of the cross—standing against the enemy in these desperate times—you need to have credibility and believability in your influence.

Too many women lack credibility even in the simplest of things, such as how they dress. I think they do it to gain attention. But is it really worth gaining a little attention if it means losing credibility and integrity as a godly woman? And is that the kind of attention you even want?

I remember one year when we took a group over to Hawaii, and I was so aware of how bad and scanty and, well, ridiculous all the girls' swimsuits were there on the beach. They were obnoxious, to be perfectly truthful. The poor men with us practically needed blinders.

My daughter, Janette, and I were sitting on a bench talking about it, and a funny thing happened. All around us girls were strutting past in the briefest of swimsuits imaginable, and we watched the faces of the fellows as they came by. One by one, we saw the guys glance up at the girls with a kind of bored expression, and then look away and keep going. I guess when there's so much of it, after a while it gets boring.

This went on for a good while. And then here came a girl about sixteen or seventeen years old wearing a T-shirt and a pair of regular shorts—not short shorts, just regular old shorts. She was walking down the beach just as cute and perky as could be. She wasn't strutting or anything—just walking. And you know what? The guys' eyes were glued on her. They watched her walk all the way down the beach. She didn't even notice. She was busy looking at something else. Janette and I said together, "Isn't that interesting?" I think it says an awful lot.

TRUSTWORTHY

Beloved sister, take this exhortation to heart. Learn to be credible in your dress, in your conversation, and in your conduct. Establish credibility in all areas. The Bible talks about the virtuous woman in Proverbs 31:11 saying, "The heart of her husband safely trusts her." Can this be said of you?

I knew of a woman once who had an affair early in her marriage. She never told her husband. But even after the affair ended, she was very, very flirtatious with men. She was adorable and everywhere she went she sent out a flirty vibe. Her husband never seemed to notice. I remember wondering about that and thinking he either didn't see or he didn't care. But eventually he did find out about the affair.

One day he exploded. He said, "From day one in this marriage you've done this. You have been flirty with every close friend I've ever had." He had been watching her all through their marriage. Now, let me ask you, do you think she could influence him spiritually? Never.

If you're married, can your husband say that he safely trusts you? If you're single, can God say that of you? Can God safely trust you in your demeanor and in your character? You'll never be the influence for God you ought to be unless you've established a trusting credibility in your character.

COURAGE

Looking back at Deborah, we see that not only was she a woman of credible character, she was a woman who knew how to encourage others. After she gave her prophecy to Barak and he came back with his ultimatum—"I'll go if you go"—she didn't say, "Now, look, Barak, this is your thing. I'll stay here and pray for you." No. She showed great courage, and it doesn't look like she hesitated even for a second. "I will surely go with you" (Judges 4:9)

You know where the word "encouragement" comes from? "En" means "with," and you know what "courage" means. You need to have courage to be an encourager. Deborah was able to offer encouragement because she had courage.

What about you? Do you feel courageous? If not, maybe you need the reminder that was given to Joshua.

> Be strong and of good courage; do not be afraid, nor be dismayed, for the LORD your God is with you wherever you go (Joshua 1:9).

We gain courage when we realize that God is always with us. And I have found that I gain courage when I obey the instructions given to Joshua in chapter 1, verse 8:

> This Book of the Law shall not depart from your mouth, but you shall meditate in it day and night.

MEDITATE ON GOD'S WORD

Now, if we're to meditate on God's Word day and night, does that mean we read the Bible at the same time we're doing the dishes, or that we drive the car with one eye on the road and one eye reading the Bible?

No, it means the Word of God is in your heart and mind. You study it in the morning and get a Scripture from the Lord for that day, and later it comes back to your mind. You think about it. You ponder the truths you find there. When a trial comes up, you search your mind for a verse that will address it. You will gain courage by meditating on God's Word, but you will also gain much more.

Psalm 1:1-3 promises this about the one who meditates on God's Word:

> Blessed is the man who walks not in the counsel of the ungodly, nor stands in the path of sinners, nor sits in the seat of the scornful; but his delight is in the law of the LORD, and in His law he meditates day and night. He shall be like a tree planted by the rivers of water, that brings forth its fruit in its season, whose leaf also shall not wither; and whatever he does shall prosper.

GO INTO BATTLE WITH GOD

Now on the day of the battle, Deborah said to Barak,

> Up! For this is the day in which the LORD has delivered Sisera into your hand. Has not the LORD gone out before you? (Judges 4:14).

In essence Deborah was saying, "This is your day, Barak. You can do it! God will help you do it!" Is this the message you give to others? Do you remind them of God's nearness and His faithfulness? And are you willing to go to battle with them?

I remember several years ago having a conversation with a man who had called our house. I was busy doing something when he called and I really didn't want to talk to him, but I sensed the Lord saying, "Just let him talk." So I did, and he began to talk to me about a troubling circumstance in his life. Finally I said, "You know, in this situation I believe that God really wants to use you."

That was met with absolute silence. Then he said, "Kay, I'm far away from God. I'm at home, but my heart is not in my home. My wife and I are really estranged, and our children are little ... it's a sad situation. God just won't forgive me. I can't receive forgiveness."

I said, "Oh, our God is the God of forgiveness. As Corrie ten Boom said, 'There's no pit too deep but what the love of Jesus goes deeper still.'" [20] He asked me if I really believed that. I said, "Yes. I've seen it happen over and over again. You can't sin so badly that God's love can't reach down to forgive you. All you have to do is confess and repent. Turn from those ways."

He said, "Oh, I have turned from those ways. I haven't been into that sin for ten years, but I just don't feel forgiven."

So I asked if I could pray with him. We prayed, and at the end of that conversation I did something very uncharacteristic for me. It must have been the anointing of the Lord. I said, "I have said everything I am supposed to say to you today. I'm going to hang up now. Good-bye." And I hung up.

He called a few days later and told me he'd been thinking about our conversation and had asked for God's forgiveness. I encouraged him to go to the believers' meeting being held Thursday and talk to a dear friend who I knew would be there—a woman who is also very much a Deborah. He did and began attending regularly.

After a time, he moved away. But he sent a letter to my friend and in it he said, "Tell Kay I'm walking with the Lord. I'm out witnessing today and my wife is right beside me."

GOD WILL USE YOU

It's so glorious when God uses you to inspire someone else. Do you know that God wants to use you this way? It's true. He wants each of us to be an influence in this world. I remember when Calvary Chapel first started when we were in a small building on Church Street. I was in my thirties and had four children at home.

Every Thursday morning I would go down to the church to meet with four other ladies for prayer. Week after week we would pray, "God, raise up soldiers of the cross. Raise up an army of men to stop the enemy's work in Orange County."

Week after week after week we prayed that. We were just a small church of thirty-five or forty people—and look what God has done in and through Calvary Chapel.

Everyone can be used by God in some way to minister to the body or to influence others. I think back to those early days during the hippie period and I remember a girl in our fellowship who had done a lot of horrible damage to her brain through drug use. She was just a shell of a girl because of it, but a beautiful girl who always wore this long, flowing hippie dress.

All she could really do was walk up to people and tell them, "I love you and God loves you." That's all she said. Sometimes she'd carry a little bouquet of sweet peas, sometimes she had roses. And she'd hand that person a flower.

Well, you would not believe how many people told us later, "I walked on those grounds and I thought, *These hippie kids ... blah, blah, blah.* And then this beautiful little girl would walk up and say 'God loves you.' She must have been an angel. She couldn't have been just a human." They said the sweetness and the tenderness of her life simply melted their hearts.

FULLY COMMITTED

God can use you. He wants to use you to encourage and inspire others. But it requires commitment on your part.

Deborah was able to inspire Barak because she herself was fully committed. In order to secure victory for the children of Israel, she was willing to lay her life on the line. She didn't do this unknowingly. She was aware of exactly how many chariots the enemy Jabin had. She knew how fierce Sisera was. But she told Barak, "I'll go with you. I'll go right out there with you to attack the enemy."

Are you like that? Will you go that last mile? Will you take that extra step—even if it is inconvenient? Even if it means you have to forego your favorite TV show? Will you write that letter or spend that time in prayer?

One of the main problems the children of Israel had was that they were not completely consecrated to God. We read that in the day of judges, "There was no king in Israel; everyone did what was right in his own eyes" (Judges 17:6).

Incomplete consecration results in incomplete effectiveness. I believe that's the same reason why the body of Jesus Christ is not as powerful today as it could be. Instead of being fully committed to our King, we do whatever is most convenient for us, and whatever doesn't cost us a denial of our flesh.

But what did Jesus say?

> If anyone desires to come after Me, let him deny himself, and take up his cross daily, and follow Me (Luke 9:23).

Deborah was able to influence others because she was fully committed. Are you committed today? Answer that question honestly.

I remember once when Chuck posed this question to a group of young people. He told them to rate their commitment to Jesus on a scale of one to ten, with ten being the best. Then he said, "If you rated yourself a four, five or six, you're in the most dangerous place of all—because you're lukewarm."

We know what God said to the Laodicean church:

> So then, because you are lukewarm, and neither cold nor hot, I will vomit you out of My mouth (Revelation 3:16).

Do you know why? Because the testimony of a lukewarm, partially-committed Christian is, "I have need of nothing. I'm fine right where I am." God despises that. He wants the hungry heart. The cold heart can come under conviction, because when it's distressed it cries unto the Lord. But the lukewarm, incomplete consecration is so neutral, it is worthless.

Deborah went out with Barak and his army, and the children of Israel had their victory over Sisera's army. Sisera himself escaped that battle—the only man to do so—but he was killed by another woman, Jael. When Sisera came and hid himself in her tent, she drove a tent peg into his temple (Judges 4:17-22). It's a gruesome story, but true. And thus, Israel's victory was complete.

PRAISE TO THE LORD

At the beginning of Judges chapter 5, Deborah and Barak sing praises to the Lord for the victory He gave them. It begins,

> When leaders lead in Israel, when the people willingly offer themselves, bless the LORD! Hear, O kings! Give ear, O princes! I, even I, will sing to the LORD; I will sing praise to the LORD God of Israel.

> LORD, when You went out from Seir, when You marched from the field of Edom, the earth trembled and the heavens poured, the clouds also poured water; the mountains gushed before the LORD, this Sinai, before the LORD God of Israel (Judges 5:1-5).

But then they sing something interesting in verse 23:

> "Curse Meroz," said the angel of the LORD, "Curse its inhabitants bitterly, because they did not come to the help of the LORD, to the help of the LORD against the mighty."

They were pronouncing a curse on those who did not join the army of the Lord, those who didn't fight valiantly in the battle against the enemy.

DOERS OF THE WORD

We have a group of people like that in our country. They're called the silent majority. Instead of joining the fight when they're needed, they do nothing. I want to strongly urge you to check yourself and make sure that when you hear the Word, you do what it says—and when you hear the Lord say, "Move," you gather the courage to move in His name. It's so easy to be one who sits and listens and agrees with everything you hear, but then ignore it.

Ezekiel 33:30-32 describes such people:

> As for you, son of man, the children of your people are talking about you beside the walls and in the doors of the houses; and they speak to one

another, everyone saying to his brother, "Please come and hear what the word is that comes from the LORD."

So they come to you as people do, they sit before you as My people, and they hear your words, but they do not do them; for with their mouth they show much love, but their hearts pursue their own gain. Indeed you are to them as a very lovely song of one who has a pleasant voice and can play well on an instrument; for they hear your words, but they do not do them.

They heard the Word, but they would not do it. Don't be like that.

YOUNG AND OLD INSPIRATIONS

Maybe you're an older woman and your response to all this is, "Well, Kay, I'm along in years. I've lived most of my life. I feel like now is the time for me to just rest and relax and let these younger women carry on the battle."

Let me tell you about my older sister, Louise. I had a conversation with her one summer while she and her seventy-one-year-old friend, Mary Jayne, were helping to direct Christian camps in Williams, Arizona.

Mary Jayne, along with some of the other retirees, did all the cooking. It's not always easy to cook for kids, you know. They cooked every meal for every child. By the time summer ended, eleven groups of young people had come through the doors of that conference center, and a large number of them had come to Jesus Christ.

My sis called to tell me about something that had happened just that morning. She said, "Oh, Honey! It's so glorious. It is so glorious." She told me about one boy, the toughest boy in the camp—and every camp has one—who would come into the meeting house and just stand there sneering.

"But just this morning he said, 'I've got to find a pastor. I've got to find a pastor.' He went up to the director of the camp with tears pouring from his eyes and said, 'Oh pastor, I need the Lord. My life is a horrible mess.'"

I said, "Oh, that blesses me so much, because I get weary and think, *Well, a little longer and that will be it for me.*"

She said, "Oh, Honey, I can't do a lot now. I just oil the joints."

You know what? She did. My sister's gift to the body of Christ was being a peacemaker. She said whenever groups of Christians get together, little eruptions would happen here and there. But she could go and talk to both sides, and the next thing they knew, they were loving and hugging each other and forgiving and carrying on just as though they'd been best friends for years. She'd say, "That's about all I can do." But her influence was much needed.

It doesn't matter if you're young or old, a career woman or a stay-at-home mom, God wants to use you to influence and inspire His people. You're needed in the body of Christ. God wants Deborahs and Jaels today—women who will stand fast and who won't compromise, women who will hold their ground against the enemy.

Father, we want to be women of conviction and determination and courage. We want to influence the people You've brought to us. We know, Lord, that when we ask You this, You will bring all of heaven to our rescue to make us Your women—the women You desire us to be, to stand up against idolatry and inspire the lost back to You, so that one day, they too may be a reflection of You.

In Jesus' name we pray. Amen.

CHAPTER

14

SHE KNOWS
HER PROTECTOR

WHEN PETER, BY THE INSPIRATION of the Holy Spirit, wrote his first letter to the church, he did so in part to prepare the church for suffering.

> Beloved, do not think it strange concerning the fiery trial which is to try you ... (1 Peter 4:12).

The Romans had not yet invaded Jerusalem or begun their horrific persecution of Christians. That was still yet to come. But Peter, by the Holy Spirit, knew the church had to be prepared for persecution. It would be a mistake to read those verses and think, *Well, that was then. It happened and it was horrible, but what does that have to do with me today?* The fact is, it has a lot to do with you.

PERSECUTION

This very minute, persecution is happening around the world against the cross of Christ. And though the adversity we face in this country is not as obvious as elsewhere, we still face our own persecution.

Persecution can take the form of living with an unsaved husband who hates the gospel of Christ. It can take the form of ridicule in the workplace or among your own family members, simply because you love Jesus and want to live for Him.

My daughter told me about a woman she knew who had to pull her son out of public school and homeschool him because he received so much abuse for wearing a cross and for praying with another boy on the school grounds. Two of his teachers had brought in books on witchcraft, and that apparently was okay, but it was not acceptable for him to live for Jesus.

Beloved, I do not know what is in store for each of us, but I know we will certainly face ridicule and persecution. If we are going to let our light shine, it cannot be avoided. The ridicule started a long time ago. In fact, it started at the trial of Jesus. And we who belong to Him can be certain this will continue right up to the moment of His return.

The world runs from any situation where they might be humiliated or persecuted. That's why they can't understand the peace of a Christian—or her joy—in the face of such treatment. But we know what the Word tells us about such trials.

> The Spirit Himself bears witness with our spirit that we are children of God, and if children, then heirs—heirs of God and joint heirs with Christ, if indeed we suffer with Him, that we may also be glorified together (Romans 8:16-17).

In the Sermon on the Mount, Jesus promised this:

> Blessed are those who are persecuted for righteousness' sake, for theirs is the kingdom of heaven. Blessed are you when they revile and persecute you and say all kinds of evil against you falsely for My sake. Rejoice and be exceedingly glad, for great is your reward in heaven, for so they persecuted the prophets who were before you (Matthew 5:10-12).

YOUR TESTING

You might be a woman who is extremely bold about sharing your faith. I pray that's the case. But if you find yourself shrinking back from giving your testimony to others, I want you to pray right now and ask the Holy Spirit to build your faith and your boldness. Ask Him to build such confidence in you that you will never again be afraid to share the hope that is in you.

As we look together at the words Peter wrote to the early church, ask God to reveal Himself anew as your Rock, your Strong Tower, your Haven in times of trouble. It's only when you know your Protector that you will be able to stand firm and immovable in the face of persecution.

A glorious promise awaits us in 1 Peter 3:12.

> For the eyes of the LORD are on the righteous, and His ears are open to their prayers; but the face of the LORD is against those who do evil.

Isn't that beautiful? Well, it is if you're not doing evil, right? And you're not, of course. That means that God is for you, you righteous thing! He's for you. His eyes are upon you, watching you—and watching out for you. He wants to show Himself strong on your behalf.

Peter continues this way:

> And who is he who will harm you if you become followers of what is good? But even if you should suffer for righteousness' sake, you are blessed. And do not be afraid of their threats, nor be troubled.

But sanctify the Lord God in your hearts, and always be ready to give a defense to everyone who asks you a reason for the hope that is in you, with meekness and fear; having a good conscience, that when they defame you as evildoers, those who revile your good conduct in Christ may be ashamed. For it is better, if it is the will of God, to suffer for doing good than for doing evil (1 Peter 3:13-17).

DON'T BE AFRAID

Are you conscious today of the fact that the enemy is out to terrorize Christians? He is. He whispers all kinds of things to you, trying to make you fearful of opening your mouth to others about the Lord Jesus Christ. We listen to those lies and then we begin to repeat them to ourselves: *It will ruin my reputation. They'll think I'm a fool. They won't have respect for me.* Before you know it, you're terrified. Satan loves that, because he knows how much that demoralizes you.

In 1 Peter 5:8 we get a vivid description of who Satan is and what he is trying to do.

Be sober, be vigilant; because your adversary the devil walks about like a roaring lion, seeking whom he may devour.

That's a frightening image. Yet Peter tells us we're not to be afraid of the enemy's terror. I will confess, at times when I've read those words and I've allowed that image of the roaring lion to enter my mind, I feel like telling Peter, "That's easy for you to say."

But the truth is, it will be easy for all of us if we acquaint ourselves with Satan's tactics and remind ourselves of the Lord's protection. If we can't do those two things, we won't be prepared for the suffering to come. When persecution falls heavily on us, we're liable to give up and go hide in a corner. And that's not God's will for our lives.

The antidote to this paralyzing fear is found in 1 Peter 3:15:

> But sanctify the Lord God in your hearts.

It is so simple and yet so profound. Sanctify the Lord God in your hearts. Instead of letting fear grip your heart, recognize the One who is Lord of your life.

Peter is drawing from Isaiah 8:12-14 in this passage.

> Do not say, "A conspiracy," concerning all that this people call a conspiracy, nor be afraid of their threats, nor be troubled. The LORD of hosts, Him you shall hallow; let Him be your fear, and let Him be your dread. He will be as a sanctuary.

SANCTIFY GOD IN YOUR HEART

The Assyrians were threatening a man by the name of Ahaz, who was the king of Judah. "We're going to wipe you out," they promised. The Assyrians then went to the king of Israel and threatened him as well (Isaiah 7:1-6).

When the king of Israel received the Assyrian's threat, he went to the king of Syria, who was an enemy to Assyria, and made an alliance with him against their shared adversary. Those two kings then went to King Ahaz and said, "Now, as king of Judah, you're going to get wiped out by the Assyrians too. You should join forces with us."

But King Ahaz said no. He felt Assyria had the stronger army, so his plan was to join forces with them.

Angry, the king of Israel and the king of Syria told King Ahaz, "All right, then. We're going to wipe you out too."

So King Ahaz is in Judah joining forces with Assyria, in absolute disobedience to God, and being threatened by Israel and Syria. In the midst of this, Isaiah the prophet hears from God. He goes to King Ahaz and tells him, "You're not to make an alliance with the enemy. You are to sanctify the Lord of hosts" (Isaiah 8:13).

Do you know who the Lord of hosts is? He's the Captain of the armies of heaven. He's God Himself, the Captain of every army, and the One who can defeat any ploy of Satan on this earth. Isaiah's message was, "Don't make an alliance with Assyria. Don't be frightened by anything they're planning to do. The armies of God will fight on your behalf. But sanctify the Lord of hosts Himself and let Him be your fear, and let Him be your dread."

"Let Him be your dread." What does that mean? It means that we're not to dread the enemy—we're to dread that we might neglect to sanctify God and make Him the Lord of our lives. It means we should fear failing to revere Christ in our hearts.

YOUR DIVINE JEWELRY BOX

Most of us have some sort of jewelry box at home. You probably have a special place where you put your jewelry and a few mementos. In my jewelry box I have Chuck's high school ring, a tie clip that belonged to my dad, a piece of my mother's jewelry, and a wristwatch my sister gave me when I graduated from high school. I have some other jewelry in there, including a pair of earrings that Janette made for me in the third grade. Have you ever seen third grade earrings? She laughs when she sees them now, but they're precious to me.

Imagine if among all those things I also had the Hope Diamond, which is among the costliest of all the world's jewels. It's a marvelous, beautifully cut gem. Now, if I could bring myself to set aside the sentimental value of all my other jewelry, which piece do you think would be the most glorious when I opened my jewelry box? How would the rest of the jewelry compare to it? They would be as nothing. Everything else would pale in comparison to that one gem, and it would be the one I would most hate to lose.

Now think of the divine jewelry box of your heart. All kinds of wonderful treasures reside in our hearts. Luke tells us,

> A good man out of the good treasure of his heart brings forth good; and
> an evil man out of the evil treasure of his heart brings forth evil. For out
> of the abundance of the heart his mouth speaks (Luke 6:45).

The treasure in your heart decides what you speak. But if you belong to Jesus, then the greatest treasure in your heart—the most awesome treasure, the most beautiful treasure, the treasure that you can never lose—is the Lord Jesus Christ Himself. When you sanctify Him in your heart, you're acknowledging Him as your most important treasure. You're enthroning Him as Lord and King.

GOD ENTHRONED IN YOUR HEART

When the Lord has this rightful place in our lives, the enemy cannot terrorize us. We may not like what the enemy throws at us. I don't know what's going to happen in the future. We may lose our lives for Jesus Christ. I can tell you that I wouldn't be happy about standing before a firing squad. I'm not some great, brave person. But I know that I will be with the Lord for all of eternity, and I know the knowledge of this is what would keep me standing.

Oh, beloved, we suffer so much when we fail to sanctify God in our hearts, when we forget that He is our Protector. If God is not enthroned in your heart, fear will be. That's how the enemy works.

I remember during one of our trips to Israel, four of us left the main group while they toured the Church of the Sisters of Zion. I knew they'd be in there for at least an hour, and Cheryl needed to buy some olive wood Bibles to take home. So we decided to go shopping and bargain for those Bibles. We did—and we got a great deal on them.

As the four of us were nearing the Damascus Gate, we turned to go outside the gate, and what we saw in front of us told us something serious was happening. Right there on the street, soldiers were standing with their guns drawn. All of a sudden we heard a very loud sound and everybody began running.

My first thought was, *It's a bomb!* Just the day before, a small bomb had exploded not far from there. It wasn't a big deal—just a small bomb. They sent a little robot in to detonate it and nobody got hurt. Still … that was my first thought.

We turned and started running toward the gate, and masses of people began pushing us. I looked at Cheryl and told her to run. She did, but when we came to the corner of a building, she turned left while I went straight. Of course, I was frantic when I found that she wasn't with the three of us. I knew I had to go back to get her. By that time, we knew someone had been shot, and everyone—Jews, Palestinians, and tourists—was panicked. And in the midst of all that chaos, the soldiers began firing tear gas.

This is the point at which it matters who is enthroned in your heart. I didn't know what to do, but I did know whom to turn to. I stopped and told my two friends to pray with me. "Lord, You have power over the enemy." That was all I prayed. But it was enough.

Running back in, I could feel the armies of the Lord with me. The first group of soldiers I encountered wouldn't let me back in, but at the moment I most needed Him to do so, God moved the heart of one soldier for me, who led me through as I was calling, "Cheryl! Cheryl! Cheryl!" And wouldn't you know, the Lord God of Israel had given Cheryl favor with a soldier too? Here they came around the corner, with his arm leading her and protecting her. He brought her straight back to Mom. Isn't God glorious? Praise His name!

GO TO THE ROCK

What's the alternative in a crisis? The other option would have been for me to think, *I've got to solve this. Satan's going to do something bad here. I have to fix this myself. Oh, where's Chuck when I need him?* But that will never do. We have to go to the Rock. We have to go to the Lord Jesus Christ. He's the Deliverer. He's the Refuge. He's the Strong Tower that the righteous run into and are safe (Proverbs 18:10).

Some of us, I fear, have opted to make alliances with the enemy. We've looked at the world and determined it's stronger than we are. We've figured that if we just cooperate a bit with it here and there, we can get through life unscathed. *If I just try not to shine my light too brightly, they'll never notice me. I'll escape their ridicule.* No, no, no! That's not the way we are to live this life. We're to live it with boldness and courage.

TRANSFORMED

It's interesting that Peter is the one who wrote this message to the church. He's the one telling us not to be afraid of the enemy's terror … and yet it was Peter who denied Jesus on the night of His betrayal. He knew what it was like to be in league with the enemy, didn't he?

He walked with Jesus; he heard what Jesus had to say. He was at the Last Supper. He was in the garden with the disciples. But when it came time to stand up for Jesus, it took just a little maidservant to cause him to betray the Lord. You'd think it would have taken something a bit more terrifying, like maybe a soldier. But no. This little maidservant looked at him and said, "You walked with Him. You're one of those Galileans." And that was enough to fill Peter with terror (Luke 22:54-60).

"Not me," he said. "Not me." Yet on the day of Pentecost, when Peter was filled with the Spirit and Jesus was crowned Lord of his life—oh, after he saw the risen Savior and had breakfast with Him on the shores of Galilee—something happened. Acts 5:26-32 shows us a courageous Peter standing boldly before the very men who had crucified Christ. The enemy's threats no longer frightened him.

Like the apostle Paul, Peter had learned to discount his life as dear to himself. When Peter and Paul were beaten, they rejoiced, praising God that they had been given an opportunity to speak for Him (Acts 5:41-42).

You might say, "Oh, those were super men." No, they weren't. They were men who had sanctified Jesus as Lord of their lives.

PRAYER FOR GUIDANCE

Back in Israel with Cheryl and the group, with chaos happening all around us, we knew we needed to leave the Old City. After going through the Damascus Gate, we had to climb a series of stairs to get up to the street level. We thought we'd be safe up there. But it wasn't long before they brought up a gurney with a body covered in a sheet. Past the gurney came a great company of women screaming and waving their arms wildly. All of a sudden we heard another pop from a gun, which turned out to be a tear gas canister. But after that came something else that sounded like a real gunshot. We knew we had to get out of there.

Yet again, not knowing which way we should go, we prayed for guidance. Just a quick prayer—"Lord, show us"—but as soon as we prayed it, a thought came into my mind. "Let's go to the Garden Tomb," I said to the others. "I know the way."

We started up the street. All around us, rushing madly, came soldiers and police cars and people running—some I was sure were terrorists—pushing right up the middle of the street. Cars were honking, people were yelling—it was just mass confusion. But we kept on, climbing up the block. When we reached the top we turned a corner and started down the street, and an Israeli woman who was there waiting for a bus stopped me and said, "Oh, please do not go down there. It is very, very dangerous." I think she thought we were headed back around in the direction of the Old City again.

"We're just going to the Garden Tomb across the street," I told her.

"Ah, that is wise. That is wise. You go there."

But as we kept walking, we needed to walk down a little to get around a bus so we could cross the street. The Israeli woman was still watching us, and apparently she didn't feel comfortable with the direction we went, because she came running after us saying, "Oh, please do not go down there!"

It wasn't until I pointed to the sign that read "Garden Tomb" that she settled down and let us go. "All right, all right," she said, finally turning and walking away. She was protecting us. It was just like God had sent us an angel to make sure we didn't wander back into danger. Now, I wasn't about to go back to the Old City, but nevertheless, I think God had that woman there to make sure.

WORSHIP IN THE QUIET

We ran up to the entrance to the Garden Tomb and then into the little bookstore that's right near the gate. The four of us were kind of out of breath from all the excitement and the realization that our lives had been somewhat in jeopardy. How good it was to be in that place! By this time it was noon, and our group was expected to meet there at 12:30.

While we waited in the garden, in the quiet of that place, I sat down at the foot of Golgotha, that mount of Calvary, and I thought about how

Jesus gave His life for me there. I looked at the empty tomb that spoke of His resurrection, and I was breathless with wonder at who He is and what He is. He is my Protector. And in the peacefulness of that moment, I worshiped my Lord.

Oh precious daughter, precious sister in Christ—let Him be Lord of your life. Sanctify Him in your heart, that He would reign there and banish all fearful thoughts from you. Know Him as your Protector today. "If God be for us, who can be against us?" (Romans 8:31).

Father, we want to give You what You rightly deserve—the place of honor in our hearts. Search our hearts, Lord, and see if there are any little compartments there that we've set aside for junk. Is there anything that needs to go? Have Your way in all these things, Father. Be the Lord of our lives. We commit them afresh to You.

In Jesus' name. Amen.

CHAPTER

15

SHE IS CONTENT

WHEN A WOMAN DELIBERATELY chooses to walk in sin and indulge in things God has expressly told her not to do, she is following what I like to call the "Eve mentality." What is this mentality? It is a way of thinking that says, "I know what's better for me than God does." At the heart of this mindset is a lack of contentment.

Think for a moment about what life was like for Eve before she sinned. God had placed her in a place of incredible beauty—a garden filled with fruit-bearing trees, flowers and all kinds of delightful foliage. God gave her permission to eat from every kind of fruit tree in the entire garden ... with the exception of just one. And it was that one tree that gave Satan the tool he needed to use against her (Genesis 2:8-25).

Contentment could have spared Eve all the grief that followed. If she had trusted God to know best for her life, if she had desired to obey His word, and if she had kept contentment in her heart, she wouldn't have sinned. If Eve's mind had been filled with thoughts about God's wonderful provision for her, if she had looked around the garden at all the beautiful things God had freely given her and had nurtured a thankful spirit for those things, she wouldn't have listened to the serpent's lies. Eve should have ignored the one tree and roamed the garden looking at all God had provided. If she had done that, she wouldn't have sinned. But Eve didn't have contentment. She let her focus rest on that one tree, that one forbidden thing (Genesis 3:1-7).

A THANKFUL HEART

Do you have a thankful heart today? Do you look around at all the wonderful, delightful things God has given you and feel content to stay right in the pasture where He's placed you? Or are you restless?

You can always tell when someone is not content to stay within the parameters God has established for them. Whether or not their minds are telling them they're not content, their behavior says it to everyone else. "I know what's best for me. I know what will bring me happiness."

When a woman is walking in that mindset, it's as if she has convinced herself she can put God off to the side and hide her behavior from Him. "I'll just do what I want for a while and God won't notice. Everything will be fine." But that's just more of Satan's deception, because things are not fine when we blatantly disobey God's Word. There's always a cost. Eve lost the garden because she lacked obedience, trust and contentment. What might you lose if you continue to follow the enemy's whispers?

Not only did Eve have the beauty of the garden to distract her away from the serpent, she also had the memory of all her walks and talks with God.

I sometimes think about Eve and I wonder, *How could she? How could she have had the benefit of walking with God and talking with Him and still have sinned like she did?* But don't we also have that intimacy with God? Even if we don't see Him face to face yet, have we not heard Him speak to us through the Scriptures, or through sermons, or through that quiet voice we hear when we're praying to Him? Yet just like Eve, we let our restlessness lead us away from God.

TOTALLY COMMITTED

It's so very important that you see Satan's tactics clearly. If Eve, living in a place of absolute beauty and perfection, could be led out of fellowship with God, how are you going to stand in this dark time where Satan is "the prince of this world" and our society is in such confusion (Ephesians 2:2)?

Think about everything that bombards your mind on a continual basis. You can't watch TV or go to a movie or even walk through the checkout stand at the market without seeing ungodly images. Awful messages hit us from all sides.

Even your Christian friends who are not fully committed to Jesus can try to persuade you to compromise with them. There's no way you will be able to escape the seduction of the world unless you are absolutely, totally committed to the lordship of Jesus Christ.

You must determine that you will obey what He tells you to do regardless of how tempting the alternative looks, and then you will be content to enjoy every good thing He has given to you.

Don't forget that the world is watching you. What do you think it tells them about God when they see you are just as restless as they are? When they see you compromising or stepping over the lines they expect to be there, it tells them that what God has given to you is not good enough.

The world knows nothing at all about contentment. For them, life is a constant search for "something more." So when they come face to face with a contented, peaceful person, that's when they see something they want, something they are lacking. But if you look just like them, you're not giving them an accurate reflection of God. You're not testifying to His abundant, generous, loving heart. You're not witnessing to them about His great providence in your life.

Sometimes I have gotten so angry with Eve when I read through Genesis 3. It's aggravating to read about her conversation with the serpent and all that happened afterwards. Not only did she eat the fruit herself, she handed some to Adam—and he ate too. So now here we are, a few thousand years later, in a world filled with all kinds of problems—heartache, corruption, poisonous snakes and ferocious lions, weeds, sickness, death. Our whole world is topsy-turvy, and Satan is the prince of the power of the air, all because one woman was not content to enjoy what God had given her. Eve's sin turned the ownership of the world over to Satan and a whole new society was ushered in. And we feel its effects today.

CHOOSE WISELY

But you know what else we feel? So often we think, *If I had been in the garden, I absolutely would not have done what Eve did.* Have you ever felt that way? We say, "I know what it is to walk with God. I know what it is to fellowship with Him. I wouldn't be foolish enough to do the same thing Eve did."

But don't we do the same thing? Each of us has the same opportunity today that Eve had. Satan tries to dialog with us like he did with her. Satan tries to tempt us with things outside of what God has permitted. We could choose contentment and obedience. Yet so often, instead of making the godly choice, we choose the Eve mentality. We listen to the lies, we allow discontentment into our hearts, and we find ourselves disobeying the God who loves us—all to the delight of the enemy who hates us. I'm sad to say, but there is a bit of Eve in us all. We could choose to ignore God.

Satan's presentation often sounds much more reasonable and sensible than God's way. If we indulge his lies, he can make the commands of God sound just as illogical and unfair to our ears as they did to Eve. That's why it's so important that we practice 2 Corinthians 10:5, which says,

> We demolish arguments and every pretension that sets itself up against the knowledge of God, and we take captive every thought to make it obedient to Christ (*NIV*).

CAPTIVATE YOUR THOUGHTS

Isn't that what Satan is trying to do? Isn't he setting himself up against the knowledge of God? But if we take those thoughts captive and give them to Jesus, He can battle the enemy for us.

When we acknowledge the voice of Satan and refuse to take those pretentious arguments captive, we allow a little seed of discontentment to grow in us. Before long, God's Word seems a little bit unreasonable, and the wisdom of the world looks a little bit more inviting. Like Eve, we are in danger then of choosing sin over obedience.

The world is ready and willing to replace God's wisdom with its own. Look what our children are up against in our public schools. It's been horrifying to me over the years to hear stories of things being taught to our young children. Abstinence is not even considered to be a reasonable option for our kids. Instead they're taught about the proper use of birth control.

They're fed lies about alternative lifestyles and told that those things are perfectly normal. They're shown films and given books and encouraged to explore anything that interests them. They get this message from their teachers and their classmates—and there are an awful lot of sophisticated kids, younger than fifth graders, who will do what they can to pass along their knowledge.

THE WORLD PUSHES IMMORALITY

The people of the world are sure they know what's best for you, and they are not shy about giving you their opinion. I remember when two of my friends got pregnant, both of whom were around the age of thirty-five. When my friends went to see their doctors, they were urged to get abortions. The doctor of one of my friends not only strongly recommended it, he was ready to set it up immediately. "Do you want me to go ahead and take care of this right away?" He gave absolutely no thought to the morality of abortion or to God's opinion about it.

Doesn't this sound like it's coming right out of the garden of Eden? It's just another way of saying, "Oh, God doesn't know what's best for you. We know what's best for you. Don't listen to those old-fashioned people who tell you that you have to be moral. God isn't interested in your happiness. We know better than God—we know what is best for you."

It's interesting to note that in these discussions about fulfillment and happiness, there's no mention of herpes, unwanted pregnancy, shame, regret or broken hearts. They don't want to bring up those unpleasant subjects. So the world continues to push their immorality and then seems surprised that despite all their education, girls are still getting pregnant. Their plan isn't working.

That's because it is not God's plan for our teenage girls. God's plan for our girls is purity. It's the same for the married women, too. Sex is a gift for the marriage relationship and it's to be kept pure and undefiled. You see, God did not forbid the sexual relationship—He put boundaries around it, for your protection and for your good. It is a right and good thing, if it is kept within those boundaries. But Satan always opposes God's plan. He does whatever he can to lure you away from contentment and into a wrong relationship.

THE WORLD DECEIVES

This is just one example of the world's corrupt influence on us. We have been cleverly led into the acceptance of all kinds of sins that God's Word speaks out against. If you're old enough, do you remember when the TV show *Bewitched* first was televised? They made it seem so harmless. Cute little nose-twitching Samantha and Tabitha were so fun and adorable.

But do you realize what it brought into our culture? It brought an acceptance of witchcraft, which we have never had in America to the extent that we do now. Our culture seems fascinated not only with witches, warlocks and wizards, but also lately with vampires. The kids just eat up the books and movies that are created around those themes. And I believe it can be traced right back to *Bewitched*. It all looked so innocent in the beginning. But sin will always look simple and harmless when it first entices you.

Don't ever be deceived into thinking that the sitcoms on TV are there just for fun and games. The world knows the best way to get a point across to people is to get them laughing. It's a clever strategy.

Again, going back quite a bit, one of the programs that did more damage to our country and opened the doors for more profanity on TV than any program I know was *All in the Family*. Do you remember Archie Bunker? Now, he was not a Christian, and they didn't portray him as a Christian, but every so often he would pop up with something that sounded like a Christian ethic. The way they handled him was so subtle. He'd say something conservative or even Scripture-based, some principle, and Mike, his son-in-law, would go, "Oh, Archie." Mike was kind of a jerk, but he was the intellectual, the one in college. Whenever he'd put

Archie down or correct him, you'd find yourself thinking, *Yeah, Archie—Mike's right. You're wrong.* Even when Archie was right, he still looked foolish. No matter what he said, he came off looking like a fool.

And what did all of that do? It swayed the audience. It didn't take long before everyone watching had the same thought: *I don't want to be like Archie Bunker.* So mentally, you moved yourself more toward Mike, the humanist intellectual. It was such a subtle bit of brainwashing.

Why would we even care what the world thinks of Christians? Why does it matter whether or not Christians are shunned? It shouldn't, you know. The woman who has settled the issue of lordship in her mind will have a much easier time putting the world in its place and keeping God in His—right on the throne of her heart. That's the woman who will be content to stay in the place of safety which God has provided for her—surrounded by every blessing and satisfied by its abundance.

STAND FIRMLY ON GOD'S WORD

Paul felt a great deal of concern for the Corinthian church. Corinth was an immoral place full of all kinds of sin and licentiousness, and Paul knew that. So he wrote to the believers there,

> For I am jealous for you with godly jealousy. For I have betrothed you to one husband, that I may present you as a chaste virgin to Christ. But I fear, lest somehow, as the serpent deceived Eve by his craftiness, so your minds may be corrupted from the simplicity that is in Christ (2 Corinthians 11:2-3).

I can understand Paul's concern, because our culture is just as wicked as Corinth was. I fear for Christian women today, that if you don't stand firmly on God's Word and ignore the enticements of the world, you could be led away from your sincere and pure devotion to Christ. Or you will take up this Eve mentality that convinces you, "I know what's better for me than God knows." Beware, when you think you stand, lest you fall (1 Corinthians 10:12). You are in a very dangerous place when you think, *I can do it. I would never turn to that. I'm okay. I'm on the right path.*

JESUS AS LORD OF YOUR LIFE

The moment you start thinking that maybe the tree isn't so bad for you after all, you've taken on Eve's thinking. That's when you begin to indulge just a little. And that's when you will lose your paradise.

What is your paradise here on earth? It's your relationship with the Lord Jesus Christ. It's your relationship with the Father—hearing Him for guidance and knowing His promises are true. When you lose that, you lose the power in your life. You lose the influence that you ought to be. Your witness dims and you don't feel that blessed communion with Jesus that you should have.

What causes you to take on the Eve mentality? It's very simple: Self has usurped the place of Christ in your life. Jesus is not Lord of your life. You've stopped obeying Him because you're no longer content to live within the parameters He has set for your life. Remember, when self gets on the throne of your life, the love of the world has crept in.

The Living Bible phrases James 4:4 in such a wonderful way:

> You are like an unfaithful wife who loves her husband's enemies [when you get the love of the world in your heart].

Isn't that descriptive? What an awful thought. But it's so true. When you make friends with the world, you are making friends with God's enemies. If you can get that image in your mind, I think it will stop you from ever letting yourself get on the throne that belongs only to Jesus.

As long as Jesus Christ is Lord in your life, self is not going to rule you. When you start to watch a TV program and you see it is full of rot, you will stop watching. Your discernment will be so keen that even in the slightest things you'll know what is godly and what is not. When a temptation begins to show itself, you will automatically turn from it and put your thoughts on Jesus.

DENY SELF AND TAKE UP THE CROSS

Satan's work is to destroy you or to neutralize you. I know so many people whose lives are on the shelf. They've stopped being any kind of godly influence on our society—and it's all due to the Eve mentality. They have allowed themselves to become discontent and they have wandered away from what they knew to be right and true. They have chosen sin over obedience. Even though they have turned from that sin and repented and found forgiveness and restoration, that glorious influence they once had in the body is gone, simply because self got on the throne of their lives instead of Jesus Christ.

Ask yourself: Is it worth all that just for momentary pleasure? Is it worth losing your influence just to chase after sin for a season?

So what is the solution? Jesus gave us the answer in Mark 8:34.

> Whoever desires to come after Me, let him deny himself, and take up his cross, and follow Me.

The cost of discipleship is not easy. It might mean pain and heartache. It might mean suffering. It might mean a broken heart. The truth is, life isn't easy for anyone, and even those who do not follow the Christian path have pain and heartache. But if you deny yourself and take up your cross and follow Him, you will have strength in your life and a joy in your heart that nothing can destroy.

DETHRONE SELF, ENTHRONE CHRIST

If you want to dethrone self, then you need to identify with Christ's death on the cross. Doing this puts self to death and robs it of the power it had over you. The warfare going on between the flesh and the spirit is intense. But God's Spirit can empower you to win that battle.

When a temptation presents itself to you, you must say, "I do not have to be in bondage to this thing. Self does not have to rule me. Christ bought my deliverance, not only from the penalty of sin, but from the power of sin." I wish I could tell you that if you commit your life to Jesus right now, this moment, you will never be tempted again. But that's not true. Satan never stops trying to dethrone Christ from your life. His attacks will continue right up until the day we put on our incorruptible bodies. That's why we have to be vigilant. We have to be on guard.

There is no other path to peace and holiness than by crowning Jesus Lord of your life. Jesus said, "I am the way, the truth, and the life." (John 14:6). That means the only way to know truth in this culture is by having Christ Lord of your life. He is the One who gives you discernment. He is the One who gives you power over sin.

Are you restless today? Maybe you're not caught up in a sin, but you're just on the run, scurrying here and there, chasing after fulfillment. Take this to heart, beloved: You will never know contentment, peace or fulfillment apart from making Jesus Lord of your life. But when you do, you'll rest. You'll find the joy and contentment your heart is secretly longing for.

When problems come up, you'll know who you can go to. You'll ask Jesus to help you make those decisions. When temptation rises up, you'll be able to talk to Jesus about that. When heartache comes, you'll let Jesus be your comfort.

Today would be a good day to take the words of Joshua to heart and make them your own. "Choose for yourselves this day whom you will serve" (Joshua 24:15).

Do it today. Choose Jesus, and crown Him as your King.

"Submission"
Not what I wish to be,
Nor where I wish to go.
For who am I that I should choose my way?
The Lord shall choose for me.
Tis better far I know.
So let Him bid me go
Or stay. [21]

Father, Your Word tells us, "Godliness with contentment is great gain" (1 Timothy 6:6). We want to be women who know contentment. We want to be witnesses to the world of Your lavish love and provision. May we keep our eyes on all that You have provided, and ignore those things You have forbidden.

We ask that by Your Holy Spirit You would keep us from the Eve mentality. May we cherish obedience over indulgence, and may we never permit self to dethrone You from our lives. Take the place that belongs rightfully to You, as King of kings and Lord of lords.

And in this world, Lord, this dark, troubled, lost, hopeless world, may we shine as reflections of Your grace and mercy and love—living reflections of Your magnificent beauty.

We ask it in Your holy name. Amen.

Footnotes

Chapter 1

[1] *My Fair Lady*, Full Length Film, Hollywood, CA: Warner Bros. Pictures Production, 1964.

Chapter 2

[2] Jonathan Edwards, "Sinners in the Hands of an Angry God," Enfield, CT, July 8, 1741.

[3] Andrew Murray, *Humility: The Journey Toward Holiness*, (Grand Rapids, MI: Bethany House, 2001).

Chapter 3

[4] "O Be Careful, Little Eyes," public domain. Source: www.childbiblesongs.com.

[5] "When I Survey the Wondrous Cross," words by Isaac Watts, 1707, music by Lowell Mason, 1824.

Chapter 4

[6] Al Bryant, *Sermon Outlines on Evangelistic Services*, (Grand Rapids, MI: Kregel Publications, 2000)

[7] Source unknown.

[8] Source unknown.

Chapter 5

[9] C. Austin Miles, "If Jesus Goes with Me," 1908.

[10] "Higher Ground," words by Johnson Oatman Jr., 1898; music by Charles Gabriel.

Chapter 6

[11] William Barclay, *The Letters of James and Peter: The New Daily Study Bible*, (Louisville, KY: Westminster, John Knox Press, 2003).

[12] Edith Schaeffer, *Affliction*, (Grand Rapids, MI: Baker Books, 1993).

[13] Ibid.

Chapter 7

[14] James Strong, *The New Strong's Complete Dictionary of Bible Words*, (Nashville, TN: Thomas Nelson, 1996).

[15] Everett Worthington Jr, PhD, Charlotte van Oyen Witvliet, PhD, Andrea Lerner, BS, Michael Scherer, MS, Forgiveness in Health Research and Medical Practice, [Online].

[16] John Powell, *The Secret of Staying in Love*, (Allen, TX: Thomas More Association, 1995).

Chapter 9

[17] The Joyful Life Bible Study is a weekly Bible study for women at Calvary Chapel Costa Mesa. For more information visit: www.joyfullife.calvarychapel.com.

[18] Hugh Steven and Chuck Smith, *The Reproducers; New Life for Thousands*, (CA: G/L Regal Books, 1972).

Chapter 13

[19] Elizabeth Barrett Browning, "How Do I Love Thee," (Sonnet 43), 1850.

[20] Corrie ten Boom with John and Elizabeth Sherrill, *The Hiding Place,* (New York, NY: Bantam Books, 1984).

Chapter 15

[21] "Submission," by C. Austin Miles and Mrs. R. R. Forman, 1934.

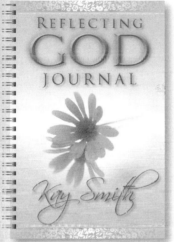

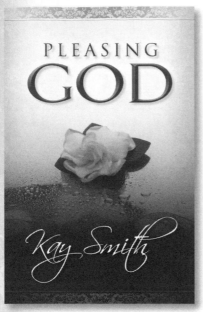

PLEASING GOD
By Kay Smith

In *Pleasing God*, Kay
Smith exhorts and
encourages women to
think of God first and
to live with His pleasure
uppermost in mind.

9781597510851

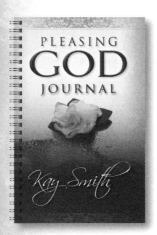

PLEASING GOD JOURNAL

Designed to be used to
accompany the *Pleasing God* book
by Kay Smith. Perfect for personal
or group women's Bible studies.

9781597510868